BRIGHT IDEAS

Reading success

CW00347810

Written by Irene Yates

Published by Scholastic Publications Ltd
Villiers House, Clarendon Avenue,
Leamington Spa, Warwickshire CV32 5PR

© 1995 Scholastic Publications Ltd
Text © 1995 Irene Yates

Author Irene Yates
Editor Christine Lee
Assistant Editor Kate Banham
Illustrator Linzi Henry
Designers Micky Pledge and Lynda Murray
Front and back covers designed by Joy White
Photograph by Martyn Chillmaid
Designed using Aldus Pagemaker
Artwork produced by Scholastic Publications Ltd
Printed in Britain by Clays Ltd, St Ives plc

British Library Cataloguing-in-Publication Data
A catalogue record for this book is available from the British
Library.

ISBN 0-590-53322-3

Contents

Introduction

Years ago, somebody sent me a quote: 'Any writer worth his salt knows that only a small proportion of literature does more than partly compensate people for the damage they have suffered in learning to read.'
(Rebecca West, *Black Lamb and Grey Falcon*, Vol 1)

That quote went straight to my heart. When I looked around the classroom I could see the 'damage' that was being done. I resolved to try to make learning to read the pleasure and the joy it deserves to be.

Learning to read is like opening a gate into a new and fulfilling world. Unfortunately not a lot of children see it as that! What they see is relentless effort and daily grind. To a good many children learning to read is something that we 'make them do in school', something to escape from as soon as possible.

In days gone by, whether you employed a 'look and say' approach, phonics, holistic language, or any other method of teaching reading, depended largely on where you were trained and the verve with which your tutor put the method across or, more likely, what resources you could muster.

Today it's not quite so cut and dried. It's widely recognised that different children have different patterns of learning and, therefore, different teaching needs. What remains constant is that learning to read, like learning to ride a bike, requires practice upon practice, and reinforcement upon reinforcement.

Riding a bike, however, is relatively easy. You get on, you fall off, you get on and try again. The incentive is huge; a whole wide world of adventure beckons, and besides, *everybody* can ride a bike, can't they?

Reading is different. You get on, you fall off, you very often don't want to try again. The pressure is great, the effort required is enormous, the incentive is practically nil. So you'll be able to read a book? So what? Why do you *need* to read books when there's a TV and a video razzmatazzing in the corner of the living room?

Besides, you just might fail. You might turn out to be one of those people who just *can't* do it – a 'slow learner', a 'special needs', one of a 'withdrawal group'. So, it might be easier to pretend you're not interested and give the whole palaver a miss.

And there, at Key Stage 1 or 2, you have an embryo reluctant reader who, if not hooked almost right away, may become a totally disaffected and absolute non-reader by Key Stage 4.

The thing to do, of course, is to stop the beginning reader 'falling off' in the first place, or, at the very least, to minimise the bruising! You have to adopt a commonsense, airy, 'Ok, pick yourself up – off we go again!' attitude – just as you would if they fell off the bike.

But how to do it? By not giving them time to think about it! The children need dozens of different activities. They need variety, flexibility and that vital practice. Above all, they need to absorb the notion that learning to read is *fun*! And, maybe, something that they're able to learn – like riding a bike – in their own special way.

You have to be open-minded. I remember Leila, who had defied every effort to teach her to read. By the time she was ten she was well and truly labelled, by herself and everyone around her. She was also a rebel and, as you would expect, a pain to have in the classroom. One day, in sheer desperation, I shoved a Junior Dictionary into her hands and told her to go away and find a word. It was something fairly obscure, like 'stealthy'. Within seconds, Leila was back, her finger on the word. I thought she'd probably got someone else to find it for her so I sent her off to search for another, and watched suspiciously.

To my amazement, Leila found the right section, ran her finger down the columns of words, and identified the word she needed.

I sent her back. Again and again. It was almost as if her mind worked backwards. If I gave her words to read, she couldn't do it. But asked to find those words in an alphabetical list, she could. What skills had she absorbed? We moved on to alphabetical lists of key words and went over and over them. Then we progressed to random lists, and then to single words on cards, always working from a 'find me the word that says ...' perspective. Until one day she realised that she could say the word before me. Leila had learned to read by a method totally her own. However, my satisfaction was nothing to the joy and triumph that Leila felt in her personal achievement.

ABOUT THIS BOOK

This book cannot tell you how to teach children to read. What it offers is a selection of activities to help you make the task varied and interesting. It isn't enough to set children off on the path to literacy – if they stop practising, they forget. A child who doesn't read, read, read, rapidly becomes a non-reader.

The book is structured in three parts: Getting them reading, Keeping them reading and Response to reading. All the activities span the age ranges and the language skills of the primary school. They are designed to be starting points, and as such can be modified in many ways to suit your pupils. They all fit in with National Curriculum requirements and you may follow them up or extend them with activities from other sections. Most of the tasks can relate to both fiction and non-fiction and can be employed across subject frontiers. Remember that 'learning to read' is about the whole curriculum not just 'English', so look for opportunities to apply the activities to other areas in the syllabus.

The word 'books' crops up frequently, as you would expect, but this is not to say the activities should just be used with 'books' – the word is used to imply texts of any kind.

Getting them reading

If there is one thing you need as a teacher of beginning readers it is *flexibility*.

The academic arguments about reading 'methods' can rage about your head and be largely ignored until somebody comes up with a fail-safe system, but you mustn't fail the children who are in your care *now*, so for the time being you must do the *very* best you can. That very best means *starting with the children*.

It is a fact that not all methods or strategies will work with all children. Some will work with most. All will work with some. But on occasions there will be a child in your class who needs a method devised all for him or herself. The better you know your children, the better your chances of success.

A large amount depends on how the children perceive reading. If it is a chore, a daily bind, something that they are being pushed to do and do and do, something in which they do not experience a great deal of success, fulfilment and satisfaction, then the whole activity will for ever remain a chore.

But if their understanding is that reading is a good way of communicating, is something that is fun and alive and full of active participation, then they will want to do it for its own sake, and the energy and drive that they put into learning to ride their mountain bikes, is the same energy and drive that they will put into learning to read.

So the classroom needs to adopt an activity-based approach to everything to do with words. It needs to be a place where ideas can be exchanged through talk, through writing, through play, through drama, through arts and crafts.

There needs to be a mountain of materials which are easily accessible – scissors, card, sugar paper, sticky tape, adhesive, coloured pencils and pens, paints. There needs to be space – for sitting, for listening, for acting out, for recording. There needs to be time – for the children to explore their own ideas and share them with others; for the children to exchange and discuss ideas, to develop and extend them, to pose questions, to go back and check, to look again, to satisfy themselves and reinforce their learning.

Story is a part of human nature. It presents us with a way of making sense of ourselves and of the world.

When they listen to a story and exchange their ideas about it with you and each other in spontaneous discussion, the children are, in effect, experiencing alternative worlds and cultures – identifying with the thoughts, feelings and actions of others in their situations and so enlarging their own understanding and perceptions.

What you read to them, how you read to them, and when you read to them is all-important. You have to be aware that what you are trying to do, at the very early stages of their awakening as readers, no matter what their age, is to inspire in them a love of books. A love of books will encourage them to want to read. And that is half the battle.

The other half of the battle is this terrible, confused process of the 'act of reading'. It is hard to put it into definitive terms. What we know is that it involves a kind of picturing, a casting back and forth of both the eye and the thinking faculty, questioning and predicting, filling in the gaps, appraisal and reappraisal, the constant search for meaning.

All of these skills, unrecognised for most of the time, need to be developed and when one or more is uncultivated it has to be looked for and strategies evolved to help the child to acquire it. This is why I say, know the children and start where they are. More specifically I should say – know the child and start where he or she is – but make the process of learning to read, above all, such an active and joyful one that it becomes a skill they are eager to accomplish.

Word bracelets

Objective
To provide a clear and easy collection of words for continuous reinforcement and recognition.

Age range
Five to seven.

Group size
Small groups or individuals.

What you need
Black felt-tipped pen, scissors, plastic shower-curtain rings, hole punch, laminating film (if available), copies of photocopiable page 113 on thin card.

What to do
Decide with the children which words it would be helpful for them to have continuous access to.

Use a black felt-tipped pen to print each word into a separate space on a copy of photocopiable page 113. Cut the rectangles out and laminate them if possible.

Punch a hole in each rectangle at the right-hand edge, then let the children thread their words on to a shower-curtain ring, reading them as they go.

Keep the word bracelets accessible at all times. Encourage the children to play games with the words, 'matching' or 'finding' or 'swapping' until they know them well, when they can exchange them for new words.

Follow-up
Add new words when necessary. You can make word bracelets for specific sets of words, for example the days of the week, the months, weather, colours and so on.

Organise competitions to find which group of children can collect the most 'bracelets' and learn the most words.

Key word groups

Objective
To promote and reinforce concepts being taught in class.

Age range
Five to eight.

Group size
Three to six children.

What you need
Card, scissors, felt-tipped pens, string, bulldog clips.

What to do
At the beginning of each half-term, make a list of key concept words which the children need to learn. These words may relate to your topic or to specific learning material. For example, if your topic was going to be 'Living things' you might choose the following as key concepts:
• mammals;
• birds;
• herbivores;
• carnivores.

Group the children and give each group one of the key concept words as its name.

Spend some time with the whole class learning more about the concepts. You might let the children take time each day to find pictures, texts or other materials which relate to their group name. Reinforce the connection between the word and what it represents as often as possible.

When the children are familiar with their name and its concept, let each group design a giant name tag. Encourage them to illustrate it to show the meaning of their name. Hang string from the ceiling and attach the designs with bulldog clips.

Sshh... not a word!

Objective
To encourage children to make up storylines for wordless books.

Age range
Five to seven.

Group size
Whole class.

What you need
A selection of wordless books, such as *The Snowman* by Raymond Briggs (Hamish Hamilton, 1978).

What to do
Young children are fascinated by books without words. Collect as many as you can. They will naturally want to make up the storylines to go with the pictures.

Start by making up some stories together to give them the idea of sequencing, using picture clues and so on. Then give them wordless books to share in pairs or small groups. Encourage them to tell their stories to each other, to you and to classroom visitors.

Follow-up
The children will get even more pleasure out of making their own wordless books. Give them plenty of time to create their storylines before they start making the books.

Build a story

Objective
To develop an understanding of, and a sense for, the concept of story.

Age range
Five to eight.

Group size
Whole class

What you need
A small object, such as a ball or a stick.

What to do
Sit with the children in a circle on the floor so that you can all see each other. Suggest an idea for a subject or a style of story. Begin the story yourself with just a few words. Pass the ball or other small object to the child on your left, encouraging him to add a few words and then pass the ball on in the same way. You may need to intervene initially to help build the story, or to let children have a turn out of sequence when they have a good idea. Be flexible about this; the best way is to let them all enjoy it.

Follow-up
When the children have had sufficient experience at building a story in this way, let them choose some of their stories to make into class books. Print the stories carefully, have the children illustrate them and help them to read them.

Big book word file

Objective
To increase familiarity with a range of frequently used words.

Age range
Five to seven.

Group size
Whole class.

What you need
Two large pieces of stiff card, sticky tape, adhesive, thin card, scissors, felt-tipped pen, 26 index cards.

What to do
Tape the two sheets of stiff card together so that they open like a book and can be stood up on the floor. Make 26 pockets slightly larger than the size of an index card and stick them inside the 'book'.

Write each letter of the alphabet on the outside of a pocket and on a card. Place the cards in the relevant pockets.

Introduce the activity by making a collection of words. Let the children choose words they encounter often in their reading and writing. Go through the list word by word and let the children take turns to fetch the right alphabet card from the pockets according to the initial letter.

Write the word, or words, on the back of the cards and keep them in the pockets. Number the words so that you can give the children a clue to which word is the one they want if it's already on the card.

Follow-up
When they are writing, encourage the children to look for words themselves before they come to ask you for them.

Telling and reading game

Objective

To develop the children's ability to interpret and organise ideas.

Age range

Five to eight.

Group size

Pairs.

What you need

Very simple short stories (which you may have written yourself) copied on to card.

What to do

Read your story from the card (pointing to the words as you go along) to one child of the pair. Then ask the child to tell the story to her partner. Ask the second child to tell the story back to you and then finally all read the card together. Decide together how close the children were to the original story.

Follow-up

This is an ideal game for involving parents. Invite them to write short family stories or anecdotes which you could print out. They could also adopt the role of principal story reader.

Make a picture-story card

Objective
To develop skills of sequencing, organisation of ideas, interpreting pictures and reading sentences.

Age range
Five to eight.

Group size
Whole class working in groups of three or four.

What you need
Old magazines and catalogues, scissors, paper, card, adhesive, felt-tipped pen.

What to do
Look in magazines and catalogues for pictures showing something happening and cut them out. (For instance, a baby equipment catalogue might show a picture of a baby being fed in a kitchen or dining room.)

Ask the children questions about the picture, for example:
- who's feeding the baby?
- what is it being fed with?
- is the baby enjoying it?
- what's the baby going to do next?
- what's mum going to do next?

When you have about six or eight responses, write them out as complete sentences. Read them with the children and let them sequence the sentences into a pleasing order.

Mount the picture and the sentences on to card. Encourage the children to think of a good title for their picture-story card, then write it at the top of the card.

Follow-up
Make lots of picture-story cards and have them accessible at all times so that the children can return to them as often as they like and share them with their friends. If possible, laminate the cards. Involve parents by getting them to look out for appropriate pictures and help their children form some sentences about them.

14

Walk, write and read

Objective
To develop picture and word matching skills.

Age range
Five to eight.

Group size
Whole class.

What you need
Camera, paper, card, felt-tipped pens, adhesive, scissors, scrapbook.

What to do
Take the children for a walk in the school grounds. Ideally you should do this at the end of each term so that you can note how the environment (and the children!) changes. During the course of the walk, take approximately six group photographs. Have these developed as large pictures if possible.

At a later date show the children the photographs and get them to remember and discuss things they saw, heard, felt, smelled and tasted on the walk. Encourage them to help you make up five or six sentences to go with each picture. Write out the sentences and stick the 'story' on to the card with its appropriate photograph.

Read and re-read the stories with the children. Mount the stories into a class scrapbook to make them easily accessible for shared reading.

Follow-up
Keep a whole year's class record of events in a scrapbook. Let the children return to it frequently. Encourage them to

compare and note changes in the environment, their own growth, and the length and complexity of their sentence stories.

Big poetry book

Objective
To encourage in the children a love of rhyme, rhythm and rich expression.

Age range
Five to eight.

Group size
Whole class

What you need
Stiff card, adhesive tape, felt-tipped pen, a selection of poems, paper or card, adhesive, easel.

What to do
Make a big book out of stiff card with paper or card pages held in place with adhesive tape.

Choose a selection of poems, paying careful attention to features such as rhyme and rhythm. Select topics and themes which group well together.

Write out the poems on white paper with a large felt-tipped pen and stick them in place in the book. Encourage the children to help you to illustrate the book and add the drawings and paintings to the poems on the pages.

Place the book on an easel so that all the children can see it. Read the poems aloud with the children and ask them to look and listen out for words that rhyme or begin or end with specific blends. Also encourage them to listen for phrases that are rich in expression.

Follow-up
Leave the big book available for free choice time and encourage the children to share it together.

Out of this world

Objective
To stimulate interest in a particular topic or theme.

Age range
Five to seven.

Group size
Whole class, divided into small groups.

What you need
Books on a variety of themes, large boxes, scrap materials, art materials, paints.

What to do
Choose a different theme for each group, for example space travel, transport, homes. Collect books and other reading materials on these themes.

Use the big boxes and the scrap materials to make a simple shape that the children can sit in to read the material about their theme. For example, children in the space travel group could make a huge rocket, while those in the transport group may like to build a lorry or a train. It doesn't have to be a complicated structure – just encourage the children to use their imagination to turn their box into something exciting.

When the children show signs of tiring with their own theme, swap them round.

Clever containers

Objective
To give lots of opportunity for browsing and enjoying reading materials.

Age range
Five to seven.

Group size
Whole class.

What you need
A variety of books, poems, reading materials.

What to do
Children who don't have access to books and reading materials, other than in school or at the Library, may have developed the idea that books always sit in neat rows on shelves. If you can offer them books in a creative way they will begin to see them as a natural part of their environment and, more importantly, view reading as an activity promoted by all sorts of ideas or activities.

Try any of the following:
• animal books could be put in a rabbit hutch, food books in a big saucepan, toy books in the doll's pram and so on;
• display books along the window-sill;
• hang books across a clothes line pinned to the wall;
• use a music stand;
• hang brightly coloured buckets from hooks on the wall.
If you don't have these resources, involve parents by inviting them to help collect items which could help with the display of books.
Discuss with the children the importance of handling the books in a caring and responsible way. Let them know that unusual storage methods mean that the books must be treated with extra care.

Grab-a-book

Objective
To establish fun reading times.

Age range
Five to eleven.

Group size
Whole class.

What you need
A wide variety of reading material.

What to do
The idea of grab-a-book time is to allow children some flexibility in the way they read and to make it fun. Establish a regular time once or twice a week when you say, 'It's time to grab a book and find a spot'.

Let the children read with their friends if they wish and swap favourite books, and generally make this a special reading time and a relaxing and enjoyable event that they can look forward to.

Finding their own spot to read in is an important part of the activity since it gives children the idea that they are reading voluntarily.

Follow-up
Establish a 'spontaneous' feedback session where the children can share what they have been reading with their peers.

Getting to know books

Objective
To create an awareness that books are available in different formats.

Age range
Five to seven.

Group size
Whole class.

What you need
A collection of different types of books, such as pop-up books, picture books, scratch-and-sniff books, wordless books, shape books, big books, mini-books and so on.

What to do
Collect as many different format books as you can. Encourage the children to bring their own books from home as well. Guide whole-group discussion, encouraging the children to describe the design and the uniqueness of each kind of book. Which ones do they like best? Which ones are the most fun, the most interesting, the most informative?

Lead them to understand that we use different kinds of books for different purposes and that not all formats are suitable for all genres.

Follow-up
Set up a table with a collection of special books (pop-ups, flaps, tabs and so on). Prepare labels reminding the children to take special care of the books. Let the children make a label of their own after choosing a book that particularly pleases them. Ask them to write one or two sentences saying what they think is special about it.

Reading box

Objective
To expose the children to a variety of genres and types of reading material.

Age range
Five to eleven.

Group size
Whole class.

What you need
Small box, art materials, small pieces of card, table, felt-tipped pen, copies of photocopiable page 114 (optional).

What to do
Decorate the box in a way that will be appealing to the children. Write the names of different types and genres of reading material on the card, for example:
- mystery;
- fable;
- pop-up;
- biography;
- drama script;
- holiday brochure;
- comic;
- poetry;
- instructions for games.

Put the cards in the box and encourage the children to add extra cards themselves as they discover new kinds of material.

Each Friday, invite one child to pull a card from the box and read out what it says. Ask the children to collect appropriate material over the course of the following week.

Ask questions such as:
- What might they bring in to class?
- Does anyone have anything suitable already?
- Where might they look for things?

Bring some material of your own in case they forget!

Set up a table for the resources and set aside some time during the week for shared reading.

Follow-up
Involve the parents in the resource collection by using photocopiable page 114. Let the children fill it in, illustrate it and take it home with them. Make a class reading diary showing the different kinds of material the children have read.

Alphabet song

Objective
To teach the alphabet.

Age range
Five to six.

Group size
Whole class.

What you need
52 pieces of card, each one showing a different letter of the alphabet, with capitals and lower case on separate cards.

What to do
Arrange the letter cards in order, so that the children can see them, then sing the alphabet several times, pointing to the letters as you go along, until the children begin to absorb it. When the children have a reasonable knowledge of the letters and the song, deal the cards out.

Play the following game, using only the names of the letters at first. Explain that as you sing a letter, the child who has it should hold it up. Make the game as much fun as possible. Then move on to singing the sounds. Tell the children the object is to sing the names and then the sounds in as fast a time as possible.

Follow-up
Make alphabet books with the children (see the following activity 'Easy as ABC').

Easy as A B C

Objective
To help children develop familiarity with the sounds and shapes of letters of the alphabet.

Age range
Five to seven.

Group size
Whole class.

What you need
A variety of alphabet books in different formats, paper, card, felt-tipped pens, textured materials, adhesive, adhesive tape, scissors, alphabet templates, old magazines.

What to do
Show the children the alphabet books. Leave the books on display over a period of time and encourage the children to read and absorb the material.

Help them to develop their own alphabet books. Make a large group or class book first to give the children the opportunity to share in creating a book. Then help them to use their own ideas to create individual books. Give them templates of alphabet letters or let them cut out letters from magazine headings. Suggest that they use themes for their alphabet books, such as animals, toys, games etc. Encourage them to develop their own ideas.

Follow-up

Display the children's alphabet books and give them time and space to share their books with each other. Encourage them to compare and contrast the books, and to give positive responses to each other's work.

Read-a-day calendar

Objective

To create an awareness of the importance of reading in our everyday lives.

Age range

Seven to eleven.

Group size

Whole class.

What you need

A copy of photocopiable page 115, a selection of books, writing materials.

What to do

Reading should very quickly become a part of children's everyday lives. The reading ideas on the calendar on photocopiable page 115 will motivate the children to read different kinds of material. You may need to adjust the activities to fit the interests and lives of your pupils. Display an enlarged copy on the wall as well as letting the children have a copy each. Ask them to cross off the activities as they complete each task.

Invite the children to write and bring in examples of reading material to share. Encourage the children to see who can think of, or bring, the most unusual pieces.

Follow-up

Ask the children to make up a new calendar. Where they can think of new items to read, pin examples to the wall, for example shopping bags, packets, advertisements, posters.

Box-snap

Objective
To develop word-matching skills.

Age range
Five to seven.

Group size
Groups of three.

What you need
Two boxes with 'windows' in, a piece of A4 card, small cards, black felt-tipped pen.

What to do
This is a simple 'snap' game for beginning readers. Write a list of words on a sheet of A4 card. Print each word again on two small cards.

Give one child the sheet of words and the others each a 'window box' and a set of cards. Explain that the child with the sheet should read out a word of her choice while the other two compete to be the first to locate the word in their sets of cards and display it in their windows. Check that the word is correct, then let them score points, two for the winner and one for the other child if he has also found the right word. No points are scored for wrong answers. The winner can be the next child to choose a word from the sheet.

Follow-up
The children can use the same cards, face down on the table to play Pelmanism or word bingo.

Find me the word...

Objective
To develop word-matching skills.

Age range
Five to eight.

Group size
Pairs or small groups.

What you need
Sugar paper, scissors, old mail-order catalogues, home-made books, card, felt-tipped pens, adhesive tape, adhesive.

What to do
Before the activity, make a book out of sugar paper to give to the pair or group.

Give the children old mail-order catalogues and ask them to cut out pictures of things they like and stick them on the pages of their books down the left-hand side. Make sugar paper pockets and stick them in place to the right of each picture. Write the name of the object on the pocket. Cut out small pieces of card to fit into each pocket and write the name of the relevant object on each one.

Spread the cards out on a table and ask the children to match them to the words on the pockets and fit them into the appropriate one.

When the children can match the words easily, cover up the words on the pockets so that they begin to read them and put them into the right pockets without matching the letters. Play 'Find me a word that says...'.

Make a big book

Objective
To develop reading and language skills by sharing the making, reading and enjoyment of a big book.

Age range
Five to eight.

Group size
Whole class.

What you need
Sugar paper, scissors, stapler or adhesive tape, a favourite book with black and white illustrations, photocopier, adhesive, felt-tipped pens, clear adhesive film.

What to do
Fold sheets of sugar paper in half and fasten them in place with staples or adhesive tape to make a basic big book. Choose a book from your collection that the children really enjoy. (The book may be photocopied for classroom only use). Copy and enlarge the pages. With the children's help, sequence the text and the illustrations. Let them colour the pictures, then stick the pages into your big book. Leave some pages at the end for the children to write or draw book reviews and other responses and stick these in. Laminate the pages of the book with clear adhesive film.

Use the book for group reading and encourage the children to share it during quiet reading.

Follow-up
• Build up a library of class-made big books and store them in a special box in the reading corner. Make them accessible to the children at all times.
• You could use the same technique, but reduce the pages on a photocopier to make a set of mini-books. However, you will have to choose carefully to ensure that the printed text doesn't become too small for the children to read.

Consonant blend snake

Objective
To encourage practice in consonant blending.

Age range
Five to eight.

Group size
Groups of three or four.

What you need
Card, small cards, felt-tipped pens.

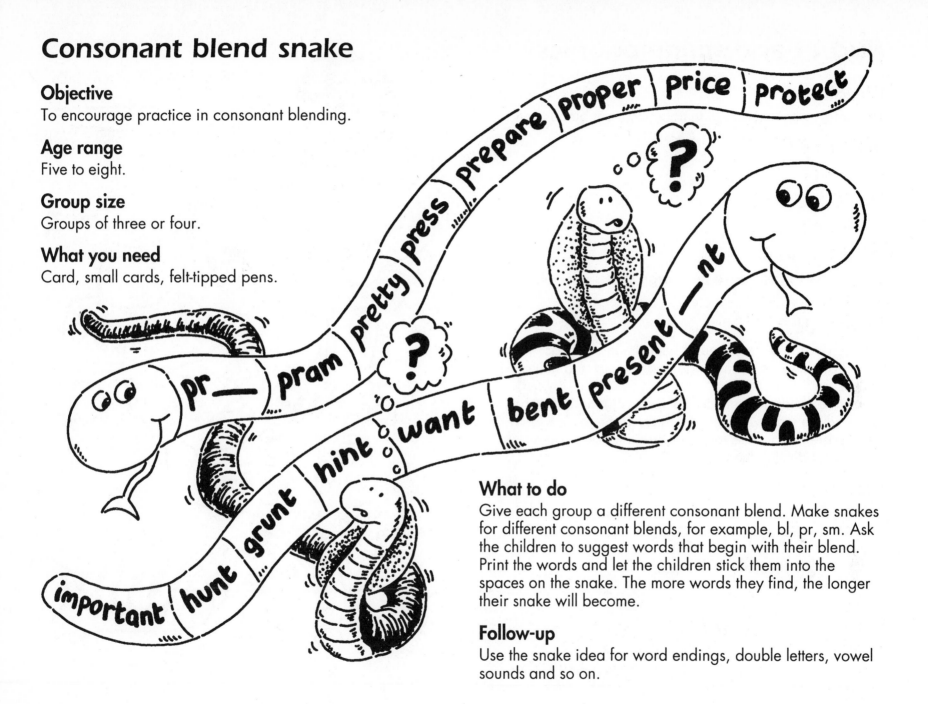

What to do
Give each group a different consonant blend. Make snakes for different consonant blends, for example, bl, pr, sm. Ask the children to suggest words that begin with their blend. Print the words and let the children stick them into the spaces on the snake. The more words they find, the longer their snake will become.

Follow-up
Use the snake idea for word endings, double letters, vowel sounds and so on.

Bucket and spade phonics

Objective
To reinforce knowledge of initial consonant blends.

Age range
Five to seven.

Group size
Whole class.

What you need
Card, scissors, felt-tipped pen, large sheets of paper, adhesive.

What to do
Cut the card into the shape of buckets and spades. Write an initial blend on each spade and a word ending on each bucket.

Ask the children to match the spades to the buckets to make whole words. When they have done this correctly, let them paste the buckets and spades on to large sheets of paper and display them.

Follow-up
Use this format to help the children with other phonic groups.

Phonic fun

Objective
To familiarise the children with different phonic letter groups.

Age range
Five to seven.

Group size
Pairs.

What you need
Card, scissors, felt-tipped pen, clear adhesive film.

What to do
This game helps to develop memory and familiarity.

Before the activity, prepare two identical sets of cards each with letters and phonic groups as in the illustration. Laminate the cards with clear adhesive film. Begin by placing the two sets of the cards face down on a surface. Ask the first child to turn over a card and sound out the letter. Then ask the second child to turn over a card and say the sound. If it matches the first one, let her take both cards. The winner is the child with the most pairs of cards at the end of the game.

When the children are confident at matching letter sounds, let them play the same game with phonic groups.

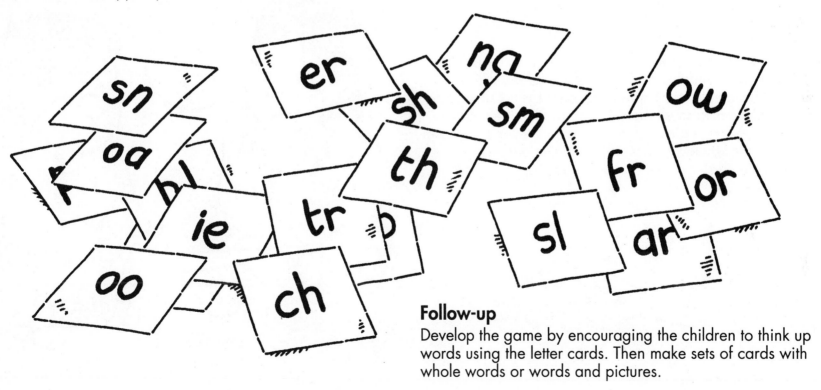

Follow-up
Develop the game by encouraging the children to think up words using the letter cards. Then make sets of cards with whole words or words and pictures.

Picture, letter, word

Objective
To develop the ability to recognise the beginning and ending sounds of words.

Age range
Five to seven.

Group size
Pairs.

What you need
Old catalogues and magazines, scissors, card, adhesive, clear adhesive film, felt-tipped pen.

What to do
Search through the catalogues and magazines for pictures of objects whose names are simple three or four-letter words, for example, sun, man, dog, egg, dish. Cut out and stick the pictures to small pieces of card. Print the initial letter on a separate piece of card, the final letter on another piece and the whole word on a third piece of card. Laminate the cards with clear adhesive film.

Spread the pictures out on a surface. Ask one child to pick a picture, then find its initial letter. Then ask the second child to find the end sound. Finally, ask them to work together to find the whole word. Make sure they are sounding out the letters and words as they go along.

The making of the cards can be a teaching activity in itself if you get the children to tell you the sounds and the words as you print them.

Follow-up
Make the game harder by spreading out the words, then get the child to read or build them and put the appropriate picture next to the word.

Sentence muddle

Objective
To support comprehension ability.

Age range
Five to eleven.

Group size
Whole class, working in teams of four or five.

What you need
A piece of text appropriate to the children's ages and reading abilities, photocopier, scissors, paper, adhesive.

What to do
Photocopy the text, then cut it up and reassemble the sentences in the wrong order and stick them in place on a separate piece of paper.

Give each team a copy of the reassembled text and ask them to read it together. Get them to cut the sentences out, discuss them, then stick them on to a sheet of paper in the order they think is correct.

Let the teams take turns to read their pieces aloud to the rest of the class. Stress that they must be able to explain why they have presented the sentences in the order they have chosen. The winning team is the one closest to the original text.

Follow-up
When the children have become familiar with the task, develop it by giving them poems with the lines out of sequence.

Word hunt

Objective
To familiarise the children with frequently used words and to develop the idea of sentence structure.

Age range
Five to seven.

Group size
Pairs.

What you need
Card, scissors, felt-tipped pen, small boxes or tins with a lid.

What to do
Print words the children need to know on to card. Photocopy the word sheet enough times so that the children can have one set each. Cut up the word sheet, and give a set of words to each child. Give the children each a small box to keep their words in.

Use the look-and-say method to teach the children a small number of words at a time, then encourage the children to reinforce their learning with each other. Ask one child in each pair to take a word from her box, read it aloud and ask the other child to 'Find me the word that says...' or 'Find the word that matches this one and read it to me'. At this point the second child should search for the matching word in her word box.

This is a good technique to use in any paired reading situation. If you are teaming older children with younger ones, they can print and make the word cards themselves.

Follow-up
As the children acquire more words, develop their learning by getting them to make up sentences for each other from the words.

Explain to parents how the game works and let the children take their word box home to play with the family. Encourage them to suggest family words to go into their boxes.

Word posters

Objective
To build up the children's word power.

Age range
Five to eight.

Group size
Individuals.

What you need
Large sheets of paper, felt-tipped pens, old magazines, scissors, adhesive.

What to do
Give each child a word, for example key words from reading resources or key concept words from other areas of the curriculum.

Explain that the children are each going to make a poster of their words. Write out the words for them in big letters, then ask each child to write a sentence containing their word. Help them with the spelling where necessary. Let them draw a picture or use cut-outs from magazines to illustrate the word.

Follow-up
Display all the posters around the classroom. Gather the children together in one group to discuss and share their words.

Sight-word bingo

Objective
To help children to improve sight-word recognition.

Age range
Five to seven.

Group size
Pairs.

What you need
Old newspapers and magazines, card, scissors, adhesive, clear adhesive film.

What to do
Choose 20 familiar words that the children use often, such as: that, which, what, when. Go through magazines and newspapers and cut out a selection of those words in a variety of different styles and sizes of print. Make 'bingo' cards by sticking 16 different words on to each card in rows of four by four. Cover the cards with clear adhesive film.

Give a bingo card and 16 small pieces of card to each pair, then play sight-word bingo by calling out words from your list of 20. Explain that the children should cover words with a small piece of card as they are called. The winners are the first pair to cover four words in a row, whether up, down, across or diagonally.

Follow-up
As the children become more confident, increase the number of words on the cards.

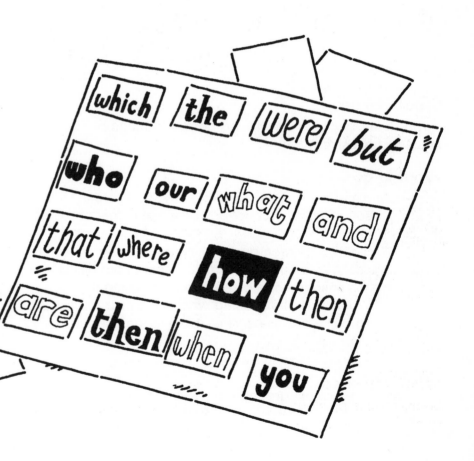

Journal exchange

Objective

To encourage children to evaluate information and apply knowledge in response to literature, to develop a sense of audience.

Age range

Five to eleven.

Group size

Whole class, working in pairs.

What you need

Books for use as journals, coloured paper, felt-tipped pens, adhesive paper shapes.

What to do

Make the children's journals look very different from ordinary school notebooks, by covering them with brightly coloured paper. Let the children make up titles for them and decorate them as they wish.

Encourage full ownership of the journals. Get the children to write stories, poems, letters – whatever they wish – in response to texts that you have read together. Encourage them to swap their journals with a partner and ask him to read what they've written and respond in writing on the pages. Keep the journals passing backwards and forwards. Explain that the readers and writers are having conversations with each other on the pages.

Join in. Be happy to respond yourself and keep your own journal to pass on to pupils.

Follow-up

Once the children are used to responding to literature in this way, encourage them to make responses to their own, and friends', writing in the same way.

Tape-a-story

Objective
To give practice in oral interpretation.

Age range
Seven to eleven.

Group size
Groups of three or four children.

What you need
Tape recorder, cassette, a quiet area.

What to do
Encourage each group to choose a book or story they wish to tape. Let them decide how they will share the reading, for example by page, chapter or paragraph. Give them plenty of rehearsal time and then help them to record their reading undisturbed in a quiet room.

Follow-up
Make a class collection of taped stories which the children can organise into a library, together with the printed texts.

Guess the book

Objective
To motivate voluntary reading of the class book collection.

Age range
Five to seven.

Group size
Groups of four or five children.

What you need
A collection of favourite picture story-books.

What to do
Before the activity, assign one child in each group the task of choosing a picture story-book with which the class is already familiar and re-reading it without the others knowing which book has been chosen.

Organise a 'guess-the-book' session, when the children ask their group's reader questions about the book and try to work out from the child's actions and answers which book was chosen. Allow one question for each child to begin with. To motivate group reading, award points or stars for good guesses. Explain to the children that the more familiar they are with the books in the classroom, the easier they will find it to play the game.

Give a different child the 'book' role for the next session. Try to ensure that everyone in the class gets at least one turn at 'being the book'.

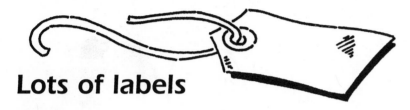

Lots of labels

Objective
To encourage reading of reference material.

Age range
Five to seven.

Group size
Groups of four to six.

What you need
Card, felt-tipped pens, bulldog clips, string, hole punch, small boxes.

What to do
When doing your year planning, make a note of some of the key concepts the children will be studying.

Give each table group the name of one of those key concepts, for example Electricity or Victorians. Encourage the groups to research into their key concept. Help them by supplying a small box of simple questions on cards to use as starting points, as in Figure 1.

Let the group design a card with their name on, then clip it to a string across the classroom. As the children do small pieces of work on their topics, display them by punching holes at the edge of the piece of work and hanging it from the card.

After a few weeks change the group names round – encourage each group to add to the card.

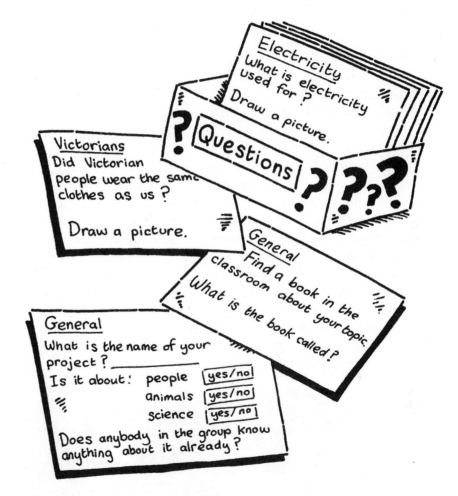

Figure 1

Choral reading

Objective
To give practice in basic skills of reading, pronunciation and expression.

Age range
Five to eleven.

Group size
Whole class, in groups of six or more.

What you need
Photocopier.

What to do
Choral reading is quite a hard skill that needs lots of practice but its achievement is its own reward, especially when it is performed for an audience. Choose a piece of text for group reading. It can be a poem, prose or any piece of writing a child has done. Copy the piece so that the children can have one each.

Explain how choral reading works and that you need to be the conductor who keeps the group together. Give each group plenty of time to read and become familiar with the piece and its meaning. Give the children lots of ideas for expression and intonation.

Allow plenty of time for rehearsal and presentation. If you can get an audience of other classes or parents, for example as part of an assembly, you will motivate the children to undertake more choral reading, and while they're enjoying it they will be practising their reading skills!

Which word?

Objective
To encourage the children to think about words.

Age range
Five to seven.

Group size
Whole class, divided into four teams.

What you need
A shoebox with a lid, a knife or scissors, small pieces of card, pencils, felt-tipped pens.

What to do
Cut a slit in the top of the shoebox, and leave the box on a table where the children can see it.

Choose a word that you want to reinforce to the children, then introduce the idea of a 'Which Word?' day. Don't tell the children which word you have chosen, but several times during the day, give them a verbal clue. Write the clue on the board or display it on the wall. An example is given in Figure 1.

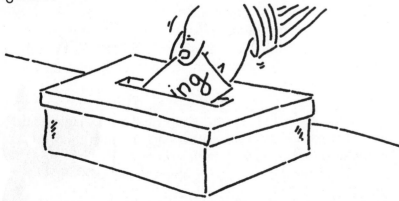

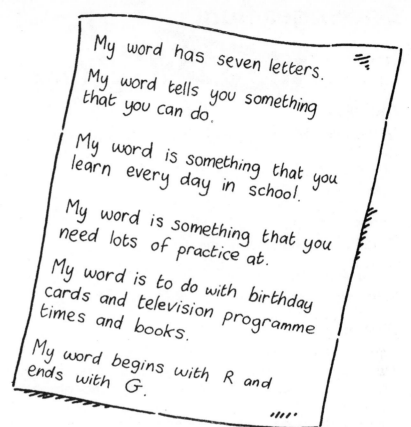

My word has seven letters.

My word tells you something that you can do.

My word is something that you learn every day in school.

My word is something that you need lots of practice at.

My word is to do with birthday cards and television programme times and books.

My word begins with R and ends with G.

Figure 1

Let the children write down their suggestions, in secret, for what the word could be and post them in the box. At the end of the day, bring the children together to go through the box and see how many in each team got the word right.

Keep a team chart and give extra points for correct spellings, meanings, explanations and so on.

Follow-up
As a variation to this game, help each team in turn to choose a word and give clues to the other teams.

Scavenger hunt

Objective
To show the children the importance of environmental print.

Age range
Five to eleven.

Group size
Variable, dependent upon the location.

What you need
Clipboard, pencil, paper.

What to do
Use every trip outside the classroom to reinforce the importance of reading. Appoint one child the recorder for the group, and arm her with a clipboard, paper and a pencil.

As you go along, look out for good examples of environmental print. Pause when you find a word or notice and ask the group's recorder to write the word. Discuss with the children the ways in which words are used to inform, to identify or to express ideas.

Encourage the children to make their own scavenger hunts for environmental print when they are out with their families and friends, and to bring their findings back to school to share with the class.

Follow-up
Post an environmental print list in the classroom for children to add to as they visit other places.

Earlybird books

Objective
To encourage response to, and sharing of, stories and books.

Age range
Five to seven.

Group size
Whole class.

What you need
A small selection of books for very young children. (These need to be the kind of books that children may have encountered in their preschool days – card books, animal books, abc books, bath books etc.)

What to do
Show the children the selection of books you have brought into school.

Discuss some of the features of the books, for example their limited words, sturdy construction, heaviness of paper or card, cloth pages, simple but colourful pictures. Ask the class what they think very young children enjoy about these books. Why are they important to children before they learn to read?

If possible, encourage the children to bring in books they have at home, to discuss and share. Set up a display and encourage exploration and browsing. Get the children to label their own books with their names so that you don't have a huge problem returning them to their rightful owners!

Time capsule

Objective
To get the children thinking about books they have read that others might enjoy.

Age range
Five to eight.

Group size
Whole class.

What you need
A large box with a lid, paper, pencils.

What to do
Ask the children to imagine that it's the year 2500 and that some archaeologists have discovered the site of their school. They are digging deep into the earth when they come across the carton which is labelled 'Class........: Favourite Books, 19...'.

Have the children brainstorm which books might be found in the box and encourage them, over the next few days, to fill the box with the suggested titles. Label the books carefully if they come from homes, libraries or other classrooms, so that they can be returned without problems.

Encourage the children to read any books they aren't familiar with. If there is time, get them to pop notes inside the books telling the archaeologists what they like about them.

What can you do?

Objective
To reinforce recognition of initial sounds and alphabetical order.

Group size
Whole class.

Age range
Five to seven.

What you need
No special equipment.

What to do
Ask the children to sit in a circle. Explain that you will go round the children in turn asking them what they can do. Tell them that they must then give an example of something they can do but the word they give has to begin with the sound of whichever letter of the alphabet is the one for their turn. For example:

Teacher: What can you do?
Child one: I can add up.
Teacher: What can you do?
Child two: I can bounce.
Teacher: What can you do?
Child three: I can count.

Keep going until you get to the end of the alphabet, then begin again, using different words.

   If a child finds it too difficult, pass on to the next child, but give the first child another chance later.

   Where there is no easily found verb for a particular letter, let the children use another part of speech so, for example, it is acceptable for a child to say for q, I can look at a

Queen. Give the children a point for each one they get right, and let them keep count of their score themselves. When you have been round the class several times, see who has the most points.

Follow-up
When the children have really exhausted initial letters, move on to initial consonant blends: st, sp, sc, sk, sl, sw, sn, sm, br, cr, dr, pr, tr, gr, fr, bl, pl, cl, fl, gl, and consonant digraphs: ch, sh, th, wh. These will have to be written on the board for the children to refer to.

Word football

Objective
To increase the child's sight vocabulary.

Age range
Five to seven, or older children with special needs.

Group size
Pairs.

What you need
A sheet of card, felt-tipped pens, smaller pieces of card, scissors.

What to do
On the sheet of card draw a football pitch with two goal posts and mark about ten lines parallel to the half way line, about an inch apart along the pitch. Draw a football on a 7cm square of card, and place it in the centre.

Write approximately 30 words (preferably nouns) you wish the children to learn to practise on smaller cards and draw a picture on the back of each card as a check for the children that they have read the words correctly.

Pile the words on the 'pitch' with the pictures facing downwards then let the children each choose which goal they are aiming for. Get them to take a word in turn and read it aloud, moving the football one space towards the goalpost for each correct word. The aim is to get the football into the goal.

Follow-up
Have several 'teams' playing at the same time and set up a knock-out competition with an ultimate 'final' match.

Involving parents – 1

Objective
To involve parents in children's reading programme.

Age range
Five to eleven.

Group size
Whole class.

What you need
Letter-writing materials.

What to do
Set up a way in which parents can become involved with children's reading. Write a letter to parents outlining ways they can help with their children's reading development. Let them know how helpful it is to the children to listen to them read daily and to keep them supplied with books, magazines and so on, which will encourage them into voluntary reading.

Find ways of involving parents, for example:
• invite them on a trip to the local library with you;
• ask for volunteers to listen to children read;
• invite them to share story time with the class;
• involve them in book displays and making art work relevant to the children's reading.

Try to establish a partnership with parents, such as a Parents and Children Read Together Club. Make it a fun time for both parents and children.

Involving parents – 2

Objective
To involve parents actively in working with beginning readers.

Age range
Five to eight.

Group size
Individuals.

What you need
Letter-writing materials.

What to do
As well as sending home a list of books the children will enjoy reading with members of their family, write to parents suggesting that they help their children's reading development by choosing extra reading material, such as recipes, which they might read and share together. They might also ask family members and friends to write notes and letters to the children which they can help them to read and reply to. Send home helpful hints throughout the year to encourage parental involvement.

Encourage the children's parents to keep a folder of small materials or texts that they have shared so that the children can return to them for reinforcement and practice.

Keeping them reading

No matter how enthusiastic the children are to start with, the biggest headache of all is keeping them reading. There's so much more for them to do, particularly in their leisure time – so much more that they find of greater interest, so much that's more active – that somehow, reading as a leisure-time activity seems to have lost its allure.

However, we know that, by whatever methods they have learned to read, constant practice is the key to developing readers. So how to get them to do it?

The greatest motivator that you have at your fingertips is your own enthusiasm. If you can show the children a real and passionate love of books, of reading for its own sake, then you'll operate as a class A1 role model. There is nothing so inspiring to children as their own class teacher's fervour – they will catch your excitement as easily as they catch a cold.

Unfortunately you may not necessarily be such a book-orientated person. However all is, most definitely, not lost. You can engender enthusiasm by taking a good look at your classroom and making sure that literature plays a very important part.

For instance, you can easily boost the significance of the books in your classroom by varying your display. Every so often, have a go at moving the books around so that they arrest the children's attention. If you can move your bookshelves to a different part of the classroom, for instance, it will cause the children to think about the books, pick them up and browse.

Don't be afraid to let the children browse; they need to develop the skills of selection, and they need to be able to flick through the pages of a book to decide whether or not it fulfils their needs. And browsing leads to reading.

Caring for books

Keep a constant check on the condition of the books in the classroom. Nothing is more off-putting than getting halfway through a book and finding a whole pile of pages missing. The experience can be enough to tell a child that reading is a complete waste of time. They might not bother to pick up another book.

The more popular a book is, the more likely it is to fall to bits in the classroom. If the title is so favoured that everybody wants to read it, replace it with a brand new copy as soon as you possibly can.

Paperbacks in particular become battered very quickly and a shabby book can be very off-putting to a child you're trying to encourage into reading. Where the cover is falling apart, why not get somebody in the class to design a new one to replace it? Even better, before the books reach that stage, why not invest in transparent wipe-clean jackets and organise a monitoring system so that the children themselves take on the responsibility for keeping the books clean?

Choosing books

Bookshops are so saturated with books for children that your greatest difficulty is often what to choose. Your main criteria must be that you remain within your budget but that you aspire to cater for all of the children. Not all children will be hooked by fiction – boys, in particular, like learning 'about things', so a wide and varied range of information and reference books is just as important as your medley of adventure, fantasy, real-life stories and so on.

But don't forget the jokes and riddles, the poems, the magazines, the short, simple picture story-books that keep the children returning to their pages over and over again with their splendid illustrations and their in-built humour.

Provided you give them enthusiasm, as rich a resource as you can muster, and the time in which to grow to love the activity, you should have no difficulty keeping them reading.

Word pattern stories

Objective
To improve confidence in reading ability.

Age range
Five to seven.

Group size
Whole class.

What you need
Stories with a repeating pattern, notebooks, pencils, felt-tipped pen.

What to do
Repetitive patterns in sentences can help children to understand sentence structure. You can use them to help you establish different concepts such as up, down, in, out and so on.

Read stories to the children that have a regularly repeating pattern, so that they get a feel for repetition. Give each child a notebook with the beginning of a sentence repeated on several pages, for example: 'Down at the bottom of the deep blue sea…'.

Discuss with the children how their sentences might end, then help them to write their endings. Let them illustrate their word pattern stories and read them to each other.

Sing-along

Objective
To practise reading skills.

Age range
Five to eleven.

Group size
Whole class.

What you need
Chalkboard, OHP or photocopied songs.

What to do
Sometimes we forget that everything the children read is helping them to develop their reading skills. We miss opportunities for cross-fertilisation as we tend to compartmentalise areas of the curriculum into subject areas and forget that they complement each other.

All children love singing and, if you can find the right tunes and lyrics, songs can be used to encourage reading. These can be anything from advertisements, through hymns, to pop songs – whatever they enjoy most. Instead of just teaching them the words of songs, give the children the words to read.

Make your singing lessons a fun time, but ensure that everybody has a good stab at reading the words before you start. Go through the words very slowly, pointing to them as you read them aloud.

Children soon learn the words of a song by heart, but a poor reader will have a wonderful sense of achievement when she can 'read' the words of a song from a page. This will motivate her to much greater effort with her other reading.

Follow-up
Once the children are confident enough, stage a concert or a musical. It doesn't have to be an elaborate production with lots of technical input and an orchestra. Look for a piece with lots of choral parts and watch the slower readers blossom as they learn to read the words!

Read together

Objective
To encourage co-operative reading.

Age range
Six to eight.

Group size
· Small groups.

What you need
Picture story-books.

What to do
Choose some picture story-books and work out how many reading parts each has, allowing for two or three narrators as well as each character. Divide the class into groups as appropriate, and give each group a book. If necessary, help them with selecting who will read each part.

Give the groups time for rehearsal and encourage them to invent voices that fit the characters. Explain that the narrators need to pay special attention to the text so that they read the tags (she said, he whispered) at the right moment.

Let the groups read out their books to each other or to another audience, such as children from other classes or invited friends and families.

Follow-up
When the children are familiar with this kind of co-operative reading, lead them on to sharing non-fiction material together. This can be divided up by looking for natural breaks such as chapters, pages and topic paragraphs.

Read your own

Objective
To develop reading and listening skills and to give confidence in reading aloud to a group.

Age range
Five to eleven.

Group size
Whole class.

What you need
Work written by the children.

What to do
Give the children the opportunity to choose their best pieces of writing. Encourage them to consider a variety of fiction, non-fiction, poetry and so on.

Sit the children in a circle and give them an order in which to read their pieces of work. Ask them to read aloud with lots of expression.

Encourage the group to make positive responses to each other's work and also to their readings.

When the children are confident in both their written work and their ability to read aloud, ask them to choose other children to read their work aloud, and operate a kind of text-exchange system.

Paired reading

Objective
To encourage shared reading.

Age range
Five to eleven.

Group size
Whole class, working in pairs.

What you need
Books, magazines, catalogues, newspapers, copies of photocopiable page 116.

What to do
Pair children according to their interests and motivations, then organise a set session for paired reading at least once a week.

Let the children choose what they will read and tell them to read a paragraph or a page each. Guide them to criticise each other's reading in a positive and encouraging way. Keep the sessions short, 20 minutes is ample, and encourage them to criticise during the reading, much as you would give feedback yourself when listening to readers. Guide them to criticise each other's reading in a positive and encouraging way. They might, for example, consider tone of voice, volume, speed and confidence.

Follow-up
Use the check-sheet on photocopiable page 116 to help the children to give each other feedback on their oral reading.

Reading pals

Objective
To give children special reading opportunities, one-to-one reading practice and experience in role-modelling.

Age range
Five to eleven.

Group size
Two classes, preferably of different ages, with the children paired.

What you need
Another class teacher who supports your reading aims, a variety of reading material.

What to do
Pair the children across the classes after discussing with the other teacher their personalities, needs and so on. Work out the times you can get the children together. Discuss the goals and activities you wish to initiate. Have a range of reading resources ready for selection when the children are paired up.

Make sure the older children understand that they are acting as reading role models, not bosses, to the younger ones. Initiate lots of classroom discussion about how a responsible rapport can be achieved. The whole session can be an active and enjoyable language and social development exercise for both classes as long as the children have all been imbued with a sense of responsibility and excitement about it.

During the sessions, have the children read to each other and share reading experiences.

Follow-up
Encourage the partners to write letters to each other, and to make books for each other.

Wet playtime reading

Objective
To give the children spontaneous reading practice.

Age range
Five to eleven.

Group size
Whole class.

What you need
Old comics and children's magazines, a large box, scissors, adhesive, varnish (optional).

What to do
Those awful wet playtimes don't need to be time wasted if you put out a plea to parents to let you have old children's magazines and comics instead of throwing them away.

Ask a couple of responsible children to sort them into sets of titles. Don't worry if there are multiple issues of some; this can be an advantage as it means children can read them together. Set up a box of comics and magazines and keep it ready to pull out of your cupboard at the first sign of rain. Encourage shared reading.

Use an old box from a supermarket and get the children to cut out some of their favourite comic strips to make a montage to decorate the outside of the box. Varnish it if possible.

Put a child or a group of children in charge of sorting and organising the comics on a regular basis so they don't get into too much disarray.

Follow-up
Groups of children might like to design and write their own comics and magazines to share with the class.

Learning about books

Objective
To promote interest in books and give children experience of book language.

Age range
Seven to eleven.

Group size
Whole class.

What you need
A wide variety of books.

What to do
All books contain information on their preliminary pages, but this is often overlooked. Show the children how these pages work.

Invite them to select a book and find the title page. Ask them to identify different information on the preliminary pages and to find the following:
• the author;
• the illustrator;
• the publisher;
• the printer;
• the year of publication;
• the ISBN;
• any dedications.

Encourage them to find different books by the same author and see if they are always produced by the same publishing house. Ask them to compare ISBNs of books:
• by different publishers;
• by the same publisher;
• in hardback and paperback editions;
• in a series.

Follow-up
Let the children create some preliminary page information for books they make themselves.

FIND OUT
Who wrote these books?
Who illustrated them?
When were the books publis
name of the pu
book printed?

GRIMTON STREET

By Hazel Bro
Illustrated by T
Picture Pr

©COPYRIGHT

For Bobby, A.G.
For Luke and Alice J.W.

1

£4.99

Other books in
this series:
Ben and the Balloon
Ben the Bandit
Bravo Ben!

Ben's Books

Printed words

Objective
To compare sizes and kinds of type used in different reading materials.

Age range
Eight to eleven.

Group size
Whole class.

What you need
A variety of different reading materials.

What to do
Encourage the children to compare sizes and kinds of print used in books and other reading materials such as newspapers, posters, comics and catalogues. Make sure they look for bold and italic print as well as ordinary roman print. Discuss why some words are in bold or italics.

Talk about some of the decorative types of print used for labels and titles. Why do the children think they were used? What kind of special effect do they give to a page?

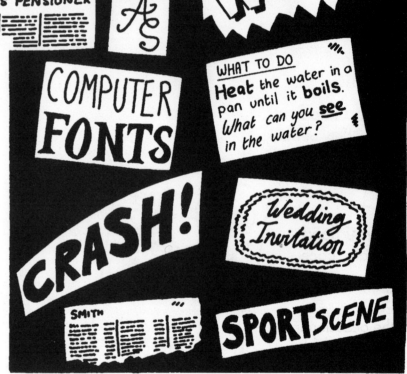

Follow-up
• Make a classroom montage of interesting print cut out from different sources.
• Give the children the opportunity to create their own decorative prints.
• Let them investigate a fonts package on the computer.

New books

Objective
To share new books together.

Age range
Five to eleven.

Group size
Whole class.

What you need
New books, paper, pencils, box.

What to do
Whenever a box of new books arrives in your classroom, turn the occasion into a very special treat. Stop whatever activities the children are doing and celebrate. Talk about the bright new covers, and crisp pages. Pass the books round carefully and let every child have the opportunity to handle them. Discuss how they will care for them and encourage the children to want to read them.

Choose children to read aloud a sample page or paragraph from each book before returning to classroom activities. Get all the children to write their names on slips of paper and choose who will read the books first by picking out names from a box.

Collect-your-own

Objective
To encourage the children to collect their own language resource material from the books they are reading.

Age range
Eight to eleven.

Group size
Whole class.

What you need
Paper, coloured card, tab dividers, stapler, pencils.

What to do
Make small, smart notebooks for the children. Use coloured card for the covers and tab dividers for the sections. Include the following sections:
- awkward spellings;
- new words;
- meanings of words;
- high frequency words;
- phrases and words from favourite poems or stories;
- 'good' words for use in writing.

Encourage the children to collect words and phrases that appeal to them or need further reference. Refer to the books often to encourage good organisation and a sense of value.

Guide the children to realise that knowledge is not just something to be consigned to memory, but is something they can organise for future retrieval.

Notebooks for new information are a particularly good way for the children to learn topic material in all areas of the curriculum. They can set up sections for history, geography, science and maths topics and use their reference book reading to add pages to their notebooks.

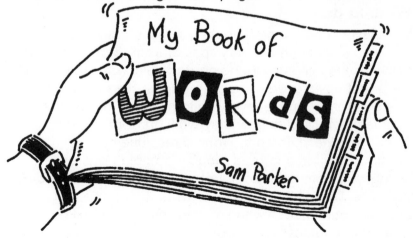

Figure 1

Language dictionary

Objective
To compile word lists in English and other languages.

Age range
Five to eleven.

Group size
Whole class.

What you need
Notebooks, pencils, rulers.

What to do
This is an especially useful technique to use in classes where there are children whose mother tongue is not English.

Demonstrate the value of all languages by getting the children to divide a page in their notebooks into columns according to the number of languages in the class. Get the children to suggest useful everyday words. Label the first column with the child's mother tongue. Label the second column English and the subsequent columns with any other languages represented in the classroom. Help the children to fill in the spaces as in Figure 1.

Follow-up
Make this a real sharing activity. Encourage the use of dual language books in your classroom and encourage exchange of languages.

Make a radio story

Objective
To enrich reading experience.

Age range
Seven to eleven.

Group size
Groups of four or five.

What you need
Story-books, self-adhesive labels (such as Post-It notes), resources for making sound effects (tins, rice, Cellophane, gravel, tray), paper, pencils, tape recorder, blank cassettes.

What to do
Ask the children to choose a favourite story and practise reading it aloud. Discuss how they can fit sound effects to it. Suggest that they can make sound effects very easily by improvising, for instance:
• rain – dropping rice on a tin lid;
• fire – rustling Cellophane;
• footsteps – walking on a tray covered with gravel;
• echo – talking into a tin.

Get the children to decide upon the kind of sound effects they need and how they could make them. Encourage them to mark places with self-adhesive labels to cue them in for when the sound effects need to happen. Discuss volume and pace with them so that they know how to pitch the effects to their best advantage.

Tape-record the stories with sound effects and listen to them as a whole class. Encourage positive responses.

Follow-up
Choose, tape and listen to some schools' radio programmes. Encourage the children to listen for sound effects. Discuss how those effects may have been made. Help them to choose further material for making their own 'radio stories'.

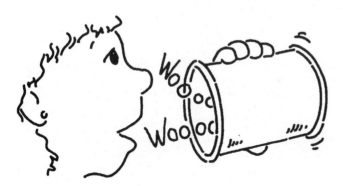

Poetry circle

Objective
To nurture enjoyment of poetry.

Age range
Five to eleven.

Group size
Whole class.

What you need
A wide range of poems.

What to do
Choose a specific time and day for the Poetry Circle and tell the children about it. Children tend to take the idea literally, so tell them that the 'Circle' will be made of chairs with no tables or desks. This will inspire enthusiasm straight away as it will be clear to the children that the session will be 'different'. Tell them that the Poetry Circle isn't a lesson, but more a kind of party where they can suggest and choose ideas. The main thing is that each child should come with at least one poem which they will have selected in advance. If children choose poems from the same book, let them sit close together to share. Make sure there is lots of fun poetry and remember that your enthusiasm will generate theirs.

Arrange the chairs in a circle – outside if the weather is good. Let the children take turns to read their chosen poems to the class. If someone is too shy to begin with, let them ask a friend to read their poem with them. Encourage a positive response from the rest of the class.

Try not to sit in judgement at their choices. It is essential to show a positive approach and to make the session an enjoyable interlude for everyone.

Follow-up
Get the children to memorise poems to recite at the next Poetry Circle meeting. They will be amazed how easy it is to learn a poem with strong rhythm and rhyme and if they can choose their own and perhaps learn them in pairs they can get quite enthusiastic. Make sure they get a good round of applause after their recitation – skim over any errors! Make the third meeting one to which they bring their own poetry for sharing.

Poetry party

Objective
To involve children in poetry reading.

Age range
Eight to eleven.

Group size
Whole class.

What you need
Poetry books, tape recorder.

What to do
Set aside a specific time and day to have your Poetry Party. Make sure a good selection of poems and poetry books is available. Before the day, record poetry programmes from schools' radio and have children practise and record their favourite poems for others to listen to.

Start the party with a listening experience, playing tapes to the children and encouraging them to discuss the way the poems are read and what they particularly like or dislike about them. Then let them write their own poems individually or in pairs and present them to the rest of the class.

Organise the Poetry Party so that the children look forward to it as a different event from their normal school day. At the party everyone should be encouraged to make some contribution, either in the form of something to be read out or by reciting from memory.

Follow-up
Have children read poems with a partner in quiet corners. Encourage them to read the poems aloud in quiet voices to help them find the rhythm and the rhyme. Help them to find creative ways of enhancing their poems, using their voices to act as orchestra or percussion by varying the pitch, pace and volume and by using non-verbal sounds for special effects. When you think they are almost ready, announce another Poetry Party.

Poetry share

Objective
To develop children's ability to select and enjoy poetry.

Age range
Five to seven.

Group size
Pairs or small groups.

What you need
A selection of poetry resources, paper, pencils, a calendar.

What to do
Post the calendar on the wall and pick three or four days in each half-term as Poetry Days. Ask the children to form pairs or groups and to pick a day when they will be the Poetry Tellers. Get them to write their names on the calendar so that they are constantly reminded when their turn will be. Don't have more than two or three groups reading on any one day.

Invite the children to select one or two poems they would like to share and copy them on to paper. Provide time during the day for the children to perform their selection of poems.

Follow-up
Provide a ring binder to collect all the poems in and label it a class poetry anthology. Keep it available for constant reading.

Topic boxes

Objective
To encourage extra reading practice at home.

Age range
Eight to eleven.

Group size
Whole class.

What you need
Shoeboxes, card, felt-tipped pens, adhesive, paper, non-fiction and fiction books.

What to do
Choose topics to go with curriculum targets, then make up topic boxes which contain as many resources as you can collect, such as reference books, pictures, photographs, objects – anything that will fit in the box. Encourage the children to collect items too – for example, shells, feathers, postcards and so on. Make some task cards related to the topic, asking questions about it, extending learning by giving information or suggesting diagrams to draw and so on. Make sure the cards are relevant to the reading resources in the box. Stick a list of the contents inside the lid of each box.

Number each box to make record-keeping easy. Give two children responsibility for signing the boxes in and out and ticking off their contents. Have the boxes available for a period of four or five days, including the weekend, so that parents can become involved with the topic 'homework'.

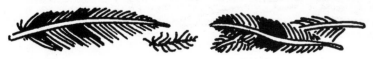

Follow-up
Encourage parents and pupils to contribute new items to the topic packs and to suggest their own ideas for packs and their contents.

Tell me a tale

Objective
To promote interest in a wide range of books.

Age range
Eight to eleven.

Group size
Whole class.

What you need
A table for display, card, felt-tipped pen.

What to do
Children are often more interested in what their peers enjoy reading than what the teacher asks them to read. Invite the children each to display on the table a book that they can recommend to others. Make a card for each book, giving the name of the child recommending it, and a few words about it. The books may be borrowed. The cards should be marked with the name of the borrower and the date, then checked off on return.

Give the children time to share their choices and discuss the merits of their books with others.

Follow-up
After reading the book, the reader can discuss and compare points with the person who recommended the book.

Share box

Objective
To spark interest and to encourage reading.

Age range
Seven to eleven.

Group size
Whole class.

What you need
Boxes, felt-tipped pen.

What to do
The more ownership the children feel, the more effort they will put into their topic learning.

Tell them the topic they are going to be working on next and suggest that they start looking out for resources. Show them the material you already have and ask them to search for books, magazine articles and so on which would be relevant.

Label a box with the topic name and ask the children to fill it. Make sure it is easily accessible. Encourage the children to discuss and to look for materials together so that they do lots of reading before the topic actually begins. Make a trip to the local library and help the children select reference material to go with the topic. Extend their knowledge of index and contents lists and point out headings and sub-headings to help them develop selection strategies so that they choose the most appropriate and useful books for their needs.

Check on the amount of reading the children have done before the topic begins. Make sure you have some new resource material to add to the box at this point.

Team book displays

Objective
To generate a sense of corporate responsibility for reading material.

Age range
Seven to eleven.

Group size
Whole class, working in groups of five or six.

What you need
Shelf or table for displays, paper, card, felt-tipped pens, scissors.

What to do
Group the children into teams of five or six and make each team responsible for a special book display once every half-term or so. Allow them to choose their own themes. They might want to group books as specific topics or books by specific authors. Provide time for careful planning and discussion.

Give them time to prepare artwork notices, labels and captions and so on. Suggest that bringing in items that relate to the theme could enhance their display. Let each team have complete ownership of their display and only intervene if they ask for your help. Let them know that they should be familiar with the books on their display so that they can answer questions about them from the rest of the class.

If possible, build a comfortable reading corner into the display area and give the children opportunities to curl up with the books they have chosen. Make the display and the corner an attractive and functional area that the children enjoy being part of.

Read-together club

Objective
To promote voluntary reading.

Age range
Five to eleven.

Group size
As many children as you can accommodate, working in groups of no more than eight.

What you need
Reading material, paper, pens.

What to do
There are times – break, lunchtime, after school – when the children see you as someone other than just 'The Teacher'. It's a great time to motivate them as they feel what they, and you, do is more spontaneous than during lesson times.

Launch a Read-Together Club to meet on a regular basis, once a fortnight or so. The meetings need to be necessarily short, say 10 to 15 minutes only. Invite the club members to bring along something short to read, such as a page from a book, a poem or a joke, and share it by reading it aloud. Insist that they keep their items short and in good taste. Make sure you always have something to share as well. Keep the emphasis on the informal and fun. Often friends will want to read aloud together something they have enjoyed. Encourage a social atmosphere and help them to find a way of deciding whose turn it is to read. Encourage children who initially want only to listen, and they may eventually find the confidence to join in.

Let the children keep a record of the club's readings and have a discussion of them now and then to bring some variety to the meeting agenda.

Classic adventure

Objective
To introduce the children to classics.

Age range
Eight to eleven.

Group size
Whole class.

What you need
Children's classic books.

What to do
The stories in classic books are timeless, and children have enjoyed them for generations.

Ask parents and grandparents if they still have any books from their childhood, and if so whether they would be prepared to loan them to the class for a short while. Set up a display of books and discuss with the children the way they are bound, their print and format and so on. Compare and contrast old classics with newer editions, for example *Alice in Wonderland, Winnie the Pooh, Wind in the Willows, Swallows and Amazons*. How do the children find them different? Which are the most inviting to read?

Choose an old and a modern abridged version of one of the classics to read aloud to the children and get them to compare the text and find differences in the use of the language. Which do they like best and why?

69

Newspaper hunt

Objective
To encourage skimming, scanning and critical skills.

Age range
Eight to eleven.

Group size
Small teams of four or five.

What you need
Paper, adhesive, scissors, newspapers.

What to do
This is a good game for developing higher order reading skills.

Hand each group a newspaper and tell them that within a specified time, for example 30 minutes, they have to cut out and stick the following items on to a sheet of paper:
- a newspaper masthead;
- a classified ad;
- a letter to the editor;
- a sports report;
- a story about children;
- a story about an animal;
- a story about somewhere that isn't local.

When they have finished, let them display their final product. Give each team points for accuracy and presentation.

Follow-up
Let the winners decide or choose eight items for a further session. Play the game several times over the school year and ensure that it gets more difficult each time by adding more items.

Read-and-add

Objective
To encourage voluntary reading.

Age range
Five to eleven.

Group size
Whole school.

What you need
A display board in the classroom or corridor, strips of paper, black felt-tipped pen, drawing pins or Blu-Tack, coloured pencils or felt-tipped pens.

What to do
Write an opening sentence of a story along a strip of paper and fasten it to your display board. The sentence might read, for example: 'One cold, dark night it began to snow in the playground...'.

Attach further strips of paper to the board with an invitation to everyone who passes to add a sentence to your story. Ask staff and visiting parents to contribute. Encourage your children to add illustrations around the sentences.

Try to build a story that stretches further than your own display board, then ask another teacher to take over when your board is full!

Follow-up
When the story is definitely finished, type it up and ask the children to illustrate it and read it out at assembly.

Adopt-a-book

Objective
To encourage care of school books.

Age range
Seven to eleven.

Group size
Whole class.

What you need
Paper, felt-tipped pens, card, scissors, adhesive tape.

What to do
It doesn't take long for books, especially paperbacks, to become 'tatty' and their untidiness often puts the children off reading them because they think the books will be dull and uninteresting.

Tell the children that books need looking after and that they are each going to 'adopt' one. Explain that to qualify, each child should choose a book to read, write a short review of it and design a new book jacket. Stress that the book jackets should be interesting and colourful, but different from the original. Their reviews could be written in the form of 'blurbs' so that they give a 'taste' of the book without giving away too much of the plot or the ending.

Help the children to cover their books with the new jackets. Place the children's reviews in a pocket on the inside cover.

Follow-up
Have a class discussion on the criteria the children use when choosing a book to read. Help them to find ways of improving their selection methods, rather than going on the initial appearance of a book.

Interest centre

Objective
To stimulate questioning, observation and word recognition.

Age range
Five to eight.

Group size
Whole class.

What you need
Objects and items related in some way to a favourite book, display table, card, felt-tipped pen.

What to do
Choose a book which all the children enjoy and know well, but which they are not yet able to read for themselves. Establish an Interest Centre in the room, displaying objects which have some connection with the book. For example, if you were reading the *Spot* books, you might set up a table with a dog's bowl, a lead, a packet of dog biscuits and a chewy bone.

With the children, work out captions for some of the objects, making sure you use vocabulary from the book. Encourage the children to watch as you write the labels, reading the words as you go along.

Let the children set up the labels with the appropriate objects, reading them aloud first. Give them lots of praise and encouragement.

Follow-up
Collect the labels up frequently and have a 'sort and read' session where the children sort through the labels, make sure they are in good condition and that they are appropriate, then put them back with the items, rewriting or replacing as necessary.

News board

Objective
To encourage children's interaction in reading and writing, to show communication in action, and to encourage them to use their initiative in devising reading material for each other.

Age range
Eight to eleven.

Group size
Whole class.

What you need
A display board, pins, card, adhesive tape, scissors.

What to do
Introduce the News Board as the children's own property. Tell them that they may use it to share any news, topics of interest, jokes, stories and so on. Each child should have ownership interest in the board and should not have to ask permission to use it. Discuss what might go on the board.

Make them responsible for updating it, putting up news items (birthdays, swaps and sales, topical items and so on).

Make some rules together about the kind of material that would be unsuitable for the board so that the children have a consensus about what is acceptable and what isn't.

Maintain the children's interest in the board. If it shows signs of flagging, put up ideas about environmental or seasonal issues, topical pieces from newspapers and so on.

Reading diaries

Objective
To encourage the children to keep personal records of their reading development.

Age range
Five to eleven.

Group size
Whole class.

What you need
Notebooks or folders with loose pages, copies of photocopiable page 117, pencils.

What to do
Explain to the children that the function of a reading diary is to keep a record of what they have read so that they can measure their own progress and maybe remind them of things they have enjoyed that they would like to read again.

Explain that if they wish they can keep very simple pages in their books, showing just the date, the title, the author, the publisher and what they thought of the book. They might also work out their own merit system so that they can award points or stars for each book they read. They might like to illustrate the pages with a scene from the book, and write a review of it when time permits. Photocopiable page 117 could be used as a basis for the reading diaries. Stress that they have complete ownership of their reading diary, and that it is not something to be read by you and 'marked', though they can share it with others as they wish.

At least once a week give the children time to write up their diaries. Every so often, allow them time to go back to them to remind them of pleasurable reading.

Follow-up
If the whole school were to adopt the concept of Reading Diaries, this would provide an excellent way of keeping the children's reading records intact throughout their school life and give a great sense of personal achievement at the end of the primary school phase.

Write a picture strip

Objective
To encourage wide reading.

Age range
Seven to eleven.

Group size
Pairs.

What you need
Children's comics, a variety of books and stories, copies of photocopiable page 118, felt-tipped pens.

What to do
The children will enjoy translating their favourite books and stories into picture strips. Show the children examples of comic strips and explain how a picture strip works. (However, children usually know exactly how to read them without being taught.) Explain that each space is called a 'frame'. Point out how the story is shown in pictures and by the use of a caption at the top or bottom of the frame, and in speech bubbles.

Choose a book or story that the children really enjoy and tell them that they are going to make it into a picture strip. Give them each a copy of photocopiable page 118, and explain that together you need to work out:
- the main characters;
- the main storyline.

Tell any children who are worried about their drawing ability that stick figures are quite acceptable. Stress that the important thing is to carry the story along through the captions and the speech. They will probably have to make some of the dialogue up. For instance, 'Rachel and her friends were excited about going to the football match' might be shown as in Figure 1.

Figure 1

After doing the first two or three frames together let the children work in their pairs to continue the story.

Follow-up
Make a class comic together for everyone to read.

Invite-an-author

Objective

To help the children understand that authors are real people.

Age range

Five to eleven.

Group size

Whole class.

What you need

No special equipment.

What to do

The first stage in arranging direct contact with an author should be to contact your local library and ascertain whether they have any plans for an author's visit in the near future. If they have, it may be possible for the author to double up the visit with some time in your school, which will obviously cut down your costs somewhat. If there is to be a local library visit, it is possible that you could get the class invited to listen to and talk with the author, at the library's expense.

The easiest way to contact authors yourself is through their publishers or through your local arts council.

If you are interested in a visit by a specific author, contact his or her publisher and ask whether the author is available for school visits, what the charge would be, and how you should arrange it. You would probably be given a contact address for the author's agent and you would make all arrangements through them.

If you are not quite so specific about your requirements, contact your local arts council by phone and ask them if they can provide you with a list of authors who could come into your school to talk to the children about writing. From the list you receive, you will be able to make a choice that fits your needs and your budget. Some arts councils have schemes for assisting you with the funding of author visits – but you usually have to ask!

To invite a poet into school, contact the Education Officer at the Poetry Society for a list of poets, some of whom may be local to your area, who are happy to make school visits. The Poetry Society will actually fund a series of poet's visits to your school through the Poets in Schools scheme (see Resources page 128 for details).

Encourage the children to think about what they want to know from the author. They should frame good, solid questions that give the author plenty to talk about. Also, stress that, as the visit is a social occasion as well as a learning experience, the children should make their guest feel comfortable, welcome and looked after.

Above all, make the visit fun for everyone involved!

Book swap-shop

Objective
To encourage children to share their responses to books.

Age range
Seven to eleven.

Group size
Whole class.

What you need
Writing materials.

What to do
Children often have books at home that they've read so many times that they would be happy to swap them with their friends.

Suggest that you organise a swap shop in the classroom where anyone can bring their old books for exchange. You need to have certain rules to ensure that nothing goes wrong. For instance, make sure the children have got parental permission to swap their books – you don't want irate grandparents coming along to retrieve the books they bought a child for her birthday! A letter home is the best way to avoid this. Just write a short letter explaining what you intend to do and provide a consent slip at the bottom to be signed by the parent.

Once a week or once a fortnight, give two or three children the task of organising the 'swap'. Make sure that they write down the titles of the books and the names of the children who are swapping. Get the children to sign their 'swap'. This ensures that if any repercussions do occur you can sort them out from the records that have been kept. Ascertain whether the children are swapping their books 'for keeps' or temporarily, and make sure that each child involved is in clear agreement on the point, but have a rule that if somebody actually changes their mind then the books should go back to their original owners.

Read-a-thon

Objective
To encourage the children to read a wide variety of books.

Age range
Five to eleven.

Group size
Whole class.

What you need
A good selection and wide variety of reading material, copies of photocopiable pages 119 and 120, prizes for the children (optional).

What to do
A Read-a-thon could be organised to raise money for replacing books in your library. Alternatively, children can be awarded points or stars for each book they read with prizes given according to the criteria you decide with them. If the children are being sponsored for money you may like to agree a maximum amount per book read so that parents don't feel under a huge obligation.

Give each child a copy of the sponsor sheet on page 119. Let them decide how many pages they will read in a month and write the number on the sheet. This way the sponsor will have an idea of what they are pledging. Get the sponsors to fill in the forms and send them back to school.

Copy the Read-a-thon Recommendation sheet on photocopiable page 120, and get the children to fill it in for each book they read. Point out that they need to show information on the sheet that proves they have actually read the book.

At the end of the month, get the children to return their sponsor sheets with the money or points they have collected. If the children are being sponsored for money, use the Recommendation sheets to decide which books to buy for the library. Encourage the children to discuss the Read-a-thon event together and decide its value for the class.

Follow-up
If the Read-a-thon goes down well with parents, try to make it an annual event.

Response to reading

The ideal, of course, is for all the reading experience of every child to be satisfying.

We would be sadly failing if we thought that this could happen – for how often have we read a book and found it disappointing? When this happens we might say to someone, 'Oh, I read in the reviews that xyz was a good book, so I bought it and... don't bother! It's trash!' 'Well, I think you would enjoy it, but it's not my cup of tea at all...'

The truth is that no two readers will take the same meaning or understanding from any book because what we bring to our reading influences what we take from it. Our experiences and feelings are all unique, so our response to the ideas presented in any book will be different from those of our peers, influenced as they are by what has gone before.

Reading is an exercise in personal choice. Can you imagine anything worse than being forced to read detective thrillers when you want to settle down with a hefty travelogue? Or being forced to read a light romance when what you really yearn to devour are the great classics?

If 34 children love a book and one hates it, we should give the one who hates it the same chance to express her very valid opinion as we give the rest of them. *All* response is about personal feeling. And so all response is legitimate.

Young readers need to be led into a situation where they can discover why their responses are as they are, and to be guided into developing ways of interacting with whatever they are reading so that this in turn will lead them to understand their own preferences. Because what we are after, ultimately, are children who will grow up to be readers in the fullest sense of the word, in whose lives the printed word has an important function, whether at work or at play.

We must provide resources and activities that nurture the children's interests and experiences, firing their imaginations, as well as furthering their development as readers. It is important to present the books we have in the classroom in ways that will keep children learning positively.

We need to be asking ourselves, at all times:
• Are the children eager to read these books, to share them with their friends? Do they discuss them enthusiastically?
• Are there materials and activities that the children find boring or unacceptable in some way? Can I weed them out, and lose them from my classroom and lessons?
• Are the children led by the activities we use for response to ask their own questions, and to suggest responses of their own?
• Are they reading widely and extensively?
• Are some of the books re-read frequently as favourites?
• Are any of the books of no interest to the children? Can the children explain why?
• Do the children show growing confidence in their reactions towards their reading material?
• Do we make time in the classroom to extend the children's literacy powers every single day?

My personal anguish is that we hardly have time to allow our children to sit back and reflect, to go back and rethink or redraft. We push them on to the sausage machine as empty sausage skins, pack them as full as we can, and push them off the other end. Some of them are at bursting point – packed with much more than their skins can contain – and others are rushed by on the conveyer belt so fast that they miss most of the packing points and fall off the end with half-empty skins.

We need to remember that some activities, to make any sense and be of any lasting value, need to be sustained over several days or even for a longer period of time. We need to respond to that sustained effort with just as much enthusiasm as we respond to the end product, in order to give our embryo 'proper' readers the fulfilment and satisfaction that will, hopefully, keep them hooked on the printed word for the rest of their lives.

Author, author

Objective
To familiarise children with authors of children's literature.

Age range
Five to eleven.

Group size
Whole class.

What you need
Photographs of authors and biographical details from book jackets and other sources, book club information, publishers' catalogues, ring binder, paper, card, scissors, adhesive, divider tabs.

What to do
Make an 'author notebook' which your children can flick through to find information about the writer whose book they are reading. Collect pictures of authors and information from book club catalogues, publishers' catalogues, professional magazines, the public library, reference books and biographies. Include as much information in your notebook as you can and add a book jacket if possible.

   Cut, trim and mount your material on to pieces of card. Place the cards in the ring binder, and use divider tabs to separate one author from another.

Follow-up
Display the appropriate pages from your binder each time you choose a different author to read to the class.

Discussion club

Objective
To encourage interactive interest in reading.

Age range
Six to eleven.

Group size
Whole class, working in small groups.

What you need
Multiple copies of a wide and varied range of books, copies of photocopiable page 121, pencil.

What to do
Set aside a specific time at regular intervals, for example once a week or once a fortnight, for a Discussion Club. You will need about an hour for each session.

Divide the class into teams and let each team choose a book to read during the period between meetings. Ask the teams to elect a different group note-taker for each session. Explain that each team is to discuss their chosen book.

The discussions should be conducted in an informal but controlled atmosphere. Make simple rules, for example:
• each child must say three things about the chosen reading material;
• the notetaker should use photocopiable page 121 and write down the best responses only, but all the group should decide which those are. Your role is to join the groups at random and help them to develop their discussion skills by posing questions, making statements and so on. Encourage them to think about specific things, for example the characters and how they relate to each other, the setting and the storyline. Ask questions such as:
• does the story move swiftly or does it get bogged down in detail?
• what category does the story fit into? Is it an adventure, a mystery, a fantasy?
• how does the story compare with others by the same author or of the same genre?
• how important and appropriate are the illustrations?

Follow-up
Make a collection of the evaluation sheets in a folder and refer back to them during the term so that groups may compare their responses to specific books.

Act it out

Objective
To acquaint children with concepts of narrative and dialogue.

Age range
Eight to eleven.

Group size
Whole class, divided into small groups. (The size will be dependent upon the material to be read.)

What you need
Multiple copies of a piece of text.

What to do
Discuss how the text can be split into narrative and dialogue. Also, look out for chunks of descriptive text which can be shared by several readers.

Give each group a story or chapter to read. Help them to choose a narrator for each group, or delegate several children to be narrators. Have other children ready to read the dialogue in role. Allow the groups freedom and flexibility to decide on who is most suitable for which role; they may wish to experiment first and decide who has the best voice and delivery for the narrator's part after their initial choice. The important thing is to give them a starting point and let them take ownership of the project.

After initial reading they need to be critical of their skills; stress that they are looking for positive points to make rather than negative. Get them to polish their delivery until it is the very best they can do.

After rehearsal, let the groups read their stories to the class or to an invited audience. Set up a 'marking' system where the groups award each other points for delivery of dialogue and narration, for expression and for confidence.

Follow-up
• When the children are familiar with the concepts of narrative and dialogue, let them work in small groups or pairs to find good texts that can be read in this way. Encourage them to write their own material together.
• Set the next project up as a competition with knock-out rounds and a final group winner.

Graphic modelling

Objective
To interpret a shared text as pictures and models.

Age range
Five to eleven.

Group size
Whole class, divided into pairs or small groups.

What you need
A favourite book, a variety of art and craft materials.

What to do
Read aloud to the class from a book they enjoy. Discuss the setting, the scenes and the characters, then allocate different episodes from the book to different pairs or groups of children. Ask them to depict the episode in the form of collage, models, pictures and so on.

Display all the scenes together to make a resumé of the book.

Follow-up
Ask the children to write short synopses of the story and display these with their work.

Script-wise

Objective
To transcribe a shared text into drama script form.

Age range
Eight to eleven.

Group size
Pairs or small groups of three or four.

What you need
A favourite book, paper, pencils, copies of photocopiable page 122.

What to do
Read aloud to the class from a book they enjoy. Discuss settings, characters and storyline, then let the pairs or groups of children choose different scenes from the book from which they should write a drama script. Explain that they need to think hard about:
- set;
- stage directions;
- dialogue.

Show them photocopiable page 122 as an example. This shows the use of stage directions and how descriptive narrative can be put into dialogue. Explain that drama script is mainly dialogue so the children will have to think about how the characters can convey in speech what is happening in the original text. This is not as simple as it might appear, but it is very challenging for them as writers.

Ensure that the original text is available for frequent reference.

Follow-up
Have specific times when the children can act out their drama scripts to each other.

Storyboard

Objective
To practise recognising the main idea and plot from a story.

Age range
Eight to eleven.

Group size
Pairs.

What you need
Story-book, large sheet of paper, pencils, felt-tipped pens.

What to do
Organise the children to work in pairs to read a story together. Explain how a storyboard is almost like a comic strip telling a story, but without being comic. It is often used by film-makers to note down the outline of a plot. It takes the outline of a story and shows it in visual terms.

Talk about the main ideas in the story and help the children to recognise the elements that make up the action of the plot.

Tell them to work together to divide their sheet of paper into 12 or 16 large squares, then choose parts of the action from the story to illustrate in each square in chronological order, so that the storyboard works as a complete synopsis of the book they've read.

Follow-up
Turn this exercise round by getting the children to create their own storyboard first, then write their own text from it.

If I were you...

Objective
To develop the ability to interpret and extend ideas from reading.

Age range
Eight to eleven.

Group size
Whole class.

What you need
Children's reading books, pens, paper.

What to do
To help the children 'get under the skin' of a character in the book they have chosen to read, set them some simple visualising and descriptive writing tasks.
• If you were the character, how would you decorate your bedroom?
• Suppose you were inviting the character home – how would you describe him/her to your family?
• If you were a reporter interviewing the character, what questions would you ask?
• Imagine you are the character and write down your thoughts and feelings in your diary.

Follow-up
The children might want to share these pieces of writing or not. Encourage sharing as far as you can, but don't insist.

Chat show

Objective
To get pupils thinking about the characters they are reading about in their books.

Age range
Eight to eleven.

Group size
Pairs.

What you need
A selection of books (fiction or non-fiction), pencils, paper, tape recorder and blank cassettes or video.

What to do
Provide the children with a varied selection of books. If you're using non-fiction books, try to find some interesting biographies that fit in with a current area of study.

Let the pairs of children choose a book from the selection and read it together. Get them to discuss the character's background and personal qualities, and how events in the book have helped to shape his or her character. Tell the children that one of them is to role-play the character, while the other will be the interviewer. The interviewer should prepare a set of questions to ask. The pair can then practise their interview before recording it on to cassette or video.

Play back the tapes or videos to the whole class so the children can discuss them and decide which were the best points of their interviews.

Follow-up
Ask the children to write up their interview as a drama script which other pairs of children can enact and develop after reading the same book.

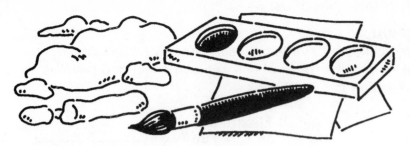

Clay characters

Objective
To help sustain motivation to read a whole series.

Age range
Five to eight.

Group size
Whole class.

What you need
A collection of books from the same series (for example, the *Little Bear* books or the *Spot* books), modelling clay, an oven, paints, card, pencils.

What to do
This strategy will help to motivate the children to read through a whole series of books.

Let the children each choose a favourite character from the series to model in clay. Encourage them to show their character in a situation from one of the stories. Bake the clay figures if possible and paint them.

Display the children's models next to their relevant books. Get the children to write a short description of their chosen character on card and put it next to the clay figure on display.

Follow-up
Let the children read their favourite stories to their clay models.

Life-size characters

Objective
To bring story characters to life.

Age range
Five to seven.

Group size
Whole class.

What you need
Chicken wire, papier mâché, old clothes and scrap materials, adhesive, paint, brushes.

What to do
You don't have to be an art and craft specialist to make a three-dimensional life-size model of one of the main characters from a book the children enjoy.

First, decide with the children which character you are going to model, then make a simple frame from chicken wire and get the children to cover it with papier mâché. Let them stick fur, feathers or wool 'hair' to it, or whatever else is appropriate. Paint the 'face' and get the children to dress the model with odds and ends of clothing.

Follow-up
Make your life-size character an integral part of story-time activities. Stand it in a special space in the classroom. Encourage the children to talk to it and about it.

Character questionnaire

Objective
To help the children observe a main character and to extract information from reading.

Age range
Eight to eleven.

Group size
Whole class.

What you need
A story you have read to the children, copies of photocopiable page 123, pencils.

What to do
Give each child a copy of the character sheet on photocopiable page 123 of this book. Show them how to fill in the sheet by going through it with them first, using a character from a story you have read to them. Then let them choose a character of their own and complete the sheet themselves. On the left hand side of the sheet the children should list personality traits of the character they have chosen (such as friendly, fearless, likes animals) and on the right hand side they should give examples or quotes from the story which show those traits, as in Figure 1.

Figure 1

Follow-up
The children could use a character sheet to fill in details of a created protagonist of their own, then write a story around their character.

Spin-offs

Objective
To retell a story from different points of view.

Age range
Seven to eleven.

Group size
Whole class, working in pairs.

What you need
Simple story, sheet of paper, felt-tipped pen.

What to do
Read the story with the children, then get them to break it down into a storyboard, showing characters, setting and plot. Divide a sheet of paper into eight to twelve squares and, beginning at the first square, draw the main events of the plot. This does not have to be complicated – the figures can be matchstick people, for instance. Drawing ability is not important, but you should stress how it is a way of organising known text.

Discuss how they could change the characters or the setting to tell a completely different story. Set them the task of telling each other the story from another character's viewpoint, or changing it in some other way. Each pair should try to have two different angles. For example, they might tell a Pooh Bear story from the point of view of Piglet or Tigger. Help them to put themselves in the situation of the character they choose, using the storyboard outline to help them stick to the plot.

Follow-up
Provide materials and time for the children to make books of the new stories and share them with the class.

Presentation corner

Objective
To encourage children to present their responses to reading material in different ways.

Age range
Five to eleven.

Group size
Whole class.

What you need
A variety of books, paper, paints, felt-tipped pens, stage block, lighting, taped music (optional).

What to do
Turn a corner of the classroom into the Presentation Corner. Make sure there is enough space for a small audience. The audience may vary from being just you, to being three or four children or half the class. Much depends, of course, on the space available! Explain that this is a place where children can present their reading in many different ways.

For example, they could:
• read dialogue aloud;
• present a puppet show;
• discuss the characters and their actions;
• dramatise scenes;
• express opinions and feelings about the story;
• read aloud a favourite section;
• present their own stories, poems or scripts written in response to the text.

Encourage the children to make picture posters of some of the books they have read and display them in the Presentation Corner.

Make the Presentation Corner an integral part of responding to reading. Give it some special facilities such as a stage block or lighting, or allow the use of taped music to open the presentation.

Multi-media workshop

Objective
To make a unique presentation of a chosen book.

Age range
Eight to eleven.

Group size
Whole class, working in small groups.

What you need
Story-book, large sheets of card, paper, pens, drawing and painting materials, camera (slides or photos).

What to do
Choose a book to read to the class over a period of time. After each reading, have a class discussion about the content of the story. At the end of the story let each group decide on a different episode to illustrate. Explain that their illustrations will build into a large mural.

Each group should then write a short piece of text to accompany its illustration. Get the children to sequence the sections and put them together to make the mural. They may need to write additional text to connect the scenes.

Take photographs or slides of each section of the mural and tape-record the children reading their pieces of writing. Present the talking slide show to other classes or to parents. Have the mural and the book on display at the same time.

Rainbow reading

Objective
To develop comprehension skills.

Age range
Eight to eleven.

Group size
Pairs.

What you need
Articles from newspapers or magazines, photocopier, highlighter pens in two different colours.

What to do
Select interesting articles from newspapers or magazines and make a copy of each article for each pair of children. Tell them to highlight the main subject of each text in one colour and three details from each text in a second colour. Ask them to give reasons for the choice of information they have coloured.

Follow-up
After some practice the children should be able to highlight additional information such as time and event chronology, cause and effect relationships and topic sentences.

Details, details

Objective
To strengthen reading comprehension skills.

Age range
Eight to eleven.

Group size
Whole class.

What you need
A shared text, paper, pencils.

What to do
Playing this game will help the children to develop their ability to state main ideas, find details and recall information.

Read a piece of text to the whole class, then ask them to write down in note form as many details as they can recall. Details can be anything that they recall from hearing the text, so they may vary from 'Jane has red hair' to 'the story is about a car crash'. Obviously the more attention the children pay, the more they will be able to recall.

Let the children take it in turn to read their list of details aloud. Explain that anyone who has the same detail on their list should cross it off. After everyone has had a turn, give the players one point for each detail not recalled by anyone else. The child with the most points should be allowed to choose the text for next time.

After several sessions, you should find their ability for sustained listening and their ability to recall are developing well. These skills will then overlap into their reading development.

Start this game with very simple, clear and literal text, building up to more complicated material throughout the year.

Follow-up
Use the game as a memory aid for knowledge-based curriculum themes.

What comes next?

Objective
To develop prediction and comprehension skills.

Age range
Eight to eleven.

Group size
Three or four children of equal reading ability.

What you need
Photocopied story.

What to do
Choose a story for group reading, but before reading the story have the children read just the title. From this, let them discuss what they think the story is about. After this discussion, let the children read silently at their own pace, but give them a predetermined stopping point such as 'third paragraph on page 5'. When they've all reached this point ask them what they think the characters will do next. Also ask them what they think the characters couldn't possibly do at the point they've reached.

Let the children read to the end of the story and then discuss whether their initial reactions to the title were borne out and what actions the characters might have taken that would have altered the course of the story.

Follow-up
Improve concentration by asking the children to find plot clues while they're reading. Ask them 'When did you first suspect that...?' or 'When did you get the idea that...?' Help them to evaluate characters, setting and plot from what they have read, through shared discussion.

Plot chart

Objective
To develop comprehension skills.

Age range
Seven to eleven.

Group size
Whole class.

What you need
Books the children have read, copies of photocopiable page 124, pencils.

What to do
This activity will help the children to clarify their understanding of the action in a story.

Explain that the action from beginning to end is called 'the plot'. There is usually a main character (SOMEBODY) who has a particular aim (WANTS something) BUT something stops that aim being achieved until the character finds a SOLUTION to the problem.

Ask the children to choose a favourite book and look for these elements of the plot:

S (somebody): Who is the main character in your story?
W (wanted): What did this character want?
B (but): But something prevented that happening. What was it?
S (solution): How was the problem solved?

Give each child a copy of photocopiable sheet 124 and ask them to fill it in as in Figure 1.

Figure 1

Follow-up
The children could create their own stories from SWBS charts when they are familiar with the way they work.

Report-a-story

Objective
To develop comprehension and reasoning skills.

Age range
Eight to eleven.

Group size
Whole class.

What you need
A selection of books, copies of photocopiable page 125, pencils.

What to do
It isn't always possible to stop and discuss the children's reading, but when they have enjoyed a book it helps them to focus their minds if they can produce some kind of feedback on it.

Have a set of report sheets (photocopiable page 125) accessible for the children. Explain that they should not feel they have to fill in a report sheet for every book they read, but some of them might like to keep their reports in a binder or a folder over the year and go back to them from time to time.

Often they enjoy going back to a book and reading it again, and actually get more out of it the second or third time round. When they do this, get them to compare their report sheets to see how much more they have discovered about the characters.

Follow-up
Some children might like to do illustrations, synopses and author biographies to go with their reports.

Story triangle

Objective
To help children focus on basic literary elements of plot, character and setting.

Age range
Seven to eleven.

Group size
Whole class.

What you need
Books or stories the children have read, a book you have read together, copies of photocopiable page 126, pencils, chalkboard.

What to do
Introduce the story triangle on photocopiable page 126. Choose a book you have read together, then demonstrate on the board how to fill in the eight lines of the story triangle as follows:
- one word, name of the main character;
- two words that describe the main character;
- three words that describe the setting (where the story takes place);
- four words telling the main character's aim in the story;
- five words telling what happened that almost stopped the main character from achieving his/her aim;
- six words telling how the main character achieved his/her aim;
- seven words describing the best part of the story;
- eight words to recommend the book to a friend.

Now give each child their own story triangle to complete using a book of their choice.

Follow-up
The children could use the story triangle to create a plan for their own stories before they write them.

Fact or opinion

Objective
To develop the ability to distinguish between fact and opinion.

Age range
Eight to eleven.

Group size
Pairs.

What you need
Card, scissors, strips of paper, felt-tipped pens, newspapers and magazines.

What to do
Cut out two pieces of card to make game boards. Label one piece 'Fact Den' and the other piece 'Opinion Den' as in the illustration. Draw boxes on the two dens to hold the facts/opinions.

Ask the pairs to look through the newspapers and magazines, and to choose some advertisements. Explain that, for each advertisement, one child in each pair should write down the name of the product and one thing about it. The other child must decide whether this is a fact or an opinon, and place the writing in the relevant den. Discuss the children's choices with them to ensure they are getting them right.

Follow-up
Once the children are used to the activity, make a point of stopping from time to time when reading narrative texts to the whole class, and asking whether specific points are facts or opinons. Discuss their responses.

Sequencing a story

Objective
To give practice in sequencing events from a known text.

Age range
Eight to eleven.

Group size
Whole class in teams of three or four.

What you need
A book that you have read to the class, paper, pen, photocopier, scissors, adhesive.

What to do
Choose ten major events from a book you have read to the children. Write a sentence that describes each of the events on a sheet of paper and photocopy it for each team. Cut out each sentence. Cut each sentence in half, muddle the sentence halves and give each team the set of muddled sentences. Explain that the children have to pair up the beginnings and endings of the sentences and stick them to a sheet of paper in the order in which the events occurred. The first team to finish and have them all correct, wins the game.

Follow-up
Pairs of children can read a book together and then set up this game for each other. Let them score points against each other for knowledge and recall. They can score a point for any sentence their partner cannot complete, or any event their partner does not remember. Make sure they check the book together to validate these points.

The dog was so excited

Mr. Brown looked up

the children took a wrong turning.

After leaving the campsite

at the broken window.

it smashed one of the windows.

Kieran threw the ball so hard

its barking woke the whole street.

Author's researcher

Objective
To develop the ability to extract information and ideas from texts.

Age range
Eight to eleven.

Group size
Pairs.

What you need
Sets of reference books, pencils, paper, stapler, card, felt-tipped pen.

What to do
Writers often hire researchers to find the information they need for their books. Set each pair a topic to write about and explain that they must decide whether to write fiction or non-fiction. Explain that one child is to be the 'Author', one the 'Researcher'. Ask them to map out a general idea of what will be in their 'book' and then decide on questions to which they need to find the answer.

Ask the 'Researcher' to find the information, write it up and give it to the 'Author', who should check it, then write the 'book'. Make sure the 'Researcher' does not try to take over the author's role.

Once they are satisfied that they know what the contents of the book will be, they can decide together on how they are going to make the book. A simple stapled-sheet format would probably be best in this instance, but make sure they leave the designing of the cover and the illustrations until the end of the task.

Display the books for the rest of the class to share.

Follow-up
Get the children to swap roles and choose another topic.

Book covers

Objective
To encourage voluntary reading.

Age range
Eight to eleven.

Group size
Whole class.

What you need
A variety of fiction, card, pencils, felt-tipped pens.

What to do
Explain to the children how the cover and 'blurb' of a book are designed to entice the reader into reading it. Sometimes the cover, the blurb and the quality of the story match; sometimes they don't.

Collect several books the children have read and discuss how the cover, blurb and story compare. Challenge them to provide new covers and blurbs for books they have read. Invite other readers to compare and contrast them.

Follow-up
Help children to develop further criteria for choosing a book to read, for example:
• choose a topic you enjoy reading about;
• read a page or two to see whether it is the right level for you;
• look for books by an author you're familiar with;
• ask the librarian to help you;
• ask for recommendations from friends.

Class reading flag

Objective
To show how much the children have achieved in reading over a year.

Age range
Five to eleven.

Group size
Whole class.

What you need
Piece of old sheeting, felt-tipped pen.

What to do
Make a flag with a piece of sheeting or curtaining that can be hung across a wall or a window. Each time a child completes a book or story that they have enjoyed, get them to write on the flag in felt-tipped pen the title and author, then add his or her signature, the date and maybe a word or two of response.

Keep the sheet folded up, but available for writing. Towards the end of the year, unfold the reading flag and hang it where everyone can see it.

Follow-up
Once the flag is on display, discuss the children's achievements with them. Give them time to read the flag, and encourage them to remember and talk about the books they have read. Give them browsing and reading time to recap on the stories they may have forgotten.

Go back

Objective
To involve the children in understanding characters in literature and to help them develop original ideas.

Age range
Eight to eleven.

Group size
Whole class.

What you need
A story that you have read to the children, pens, paper.

What to do
Encourage the children to talk about the daily life of the main character in the story and to note all the instances where they can identify with that character. Ask them to discuss the things they think shaped the character's personality. What kinds of things might the character have done earlier in his or her life.

Ask them to extend the story by imagining what might have happened before the beginning and by predicting the character's future after the story ends.

Follow-up
Get the children to work on further adventures the character might have and to present them as class, or group, books.

Sherlock! It's teatime!

Writing reviews

Objective
To develop the ability to analyse, summarise and evaluate reading material.

Age range
Eight to eleven.

Group size
Whole class.

What you need
A book that you have read to the class, writing materials, magazines which contain reviews.

What to do
Show the children review columns in magazines or comics. They will probably be most interested in music, film, video and computer game reviews at this point. Show how the writer has identified his/her audience to write the review.

Set up a Review Board on one of your display walls. Ask the children to imagine they are the Book Critic for a library magazine and to review a book you have all read. They may need to work in pairs at first to organise their ideas and remind each other of the story's main points. Stress that good report writing is brief but conveys the point effectively.

Let them share their reviews with the rest of the class and discuss their responses to the book.

Follow-up
Start a collection of book reviews in a ring-binder. Try to include reviews for all your classroom books so that new readers can refer to them before or after reading a book to see how the review compares with their own judgements.

Reading poetry

Objective
To motivate interest in reading poetry.

Age range
Eight to eleven.

Group size
Whole class.

What you need
An interesting poem, a photocopier, chalkboard or overhead projector.

What to do
Select a poem that has plenty of pace, rhythm and a good, strong narrative. Make sure all the children can see the poem either by giving them each a photocopy, writing it out on the chalkboard or showing it on an overhead projector.

Have the class read the poem together. Then vary the approach to the reading by:
• having one group read the first two lines, a second group read the next two lines and so on;
• having a group lightly tapping out the rhythm with their hands;
• having individuals reading some lines and groups reading others.

Let the children suggest ideas for enhancing the presentation of the poem.

Follow-up
Look for poems that the children could set to percussion. Remember that percussion doesn't necessarily mean musical instruments, but could be voices, hands, feet and so on.

Showing and telling

Objective
To encourage the children to verbalise their responses to a book.

Age range
Five to eight.

Group size
Whole class.

What you need
A wide selection of books, display materials.

What to do
Make a showing-and-telling session a regular part of the day's pattern. Encourage the children from the earliest stages to bring in items from home that they think will interest their peers. During a quiet period the child with the item should present it to the rest of the class.

When the children are used to show-and-tell with their own possessions, lead them into showing and talking about the books that they have read. Encourage the 'audience' to ask questions (What happened to...? Where is the story set...? What did you think of...?).

Try to set up interesting situations where two children who have read the same book but have different opinions of it are leading the session. Other children could be encouraged to volunteer to read the book and make their own judgement.

List the books that the children have used for showing-and-telling on the wall, and encourage them to choose different ones.

The great book prize

Objective
To encourage children to express their feelings and responses to books.

Age range
Eight to eleven.

Group size
Whole class.

What you need
A good selection of books, copies of photocopiable page 127.

What to do
Explain to the children that books are sometimes given awards for their merit. Among the awards given to children's books are:
• The Smarties Prize;
• The Kathleen Fidler Award;
• The Hans Christian Andersen Award;
• The Guardian Children's Fiction Award.
Tell the children how each prize has its own criteria for selection.

Encourage the children to think up their own ideas for awards, for example:
• best illustrated book;
• best adventure book;
• best humorous book.

Suggest that they might like to use their own name for the award, for instance The Jones Award, The Sophie Award or The Sameer Prize. Distribute copies of photocopiable page 127 to use as a starting point to design the awards.

Give the children a minimum number of books they must read in order to make their choice. Stress that they need to read each book thoroughly and keep some kind of record of their reading, showing good points and making special remarks, so that they can decide which book their award will go to.

Follow-up
Why not give a Class Book Award of the Month? This would entail lots of discussion and comparison. Contenders could be written up clearly on a sheet of paper on the wall so that everyone could have a chance to read them before making a final vote.

Reading between the lines

Objective
To get the children looking closely at meaning and expression.

Age range
Nine to eleven.

Group size
Three to five.

What you need
A varied selection of newspapers, all carrying versions of the same news item.

What to do
Introduce the children to the idea that the same 'story', whether a news item or a sports review, might be presented in very different ways.

Ask them to look in different newspapers for versions of the same story. Explain that you are going to ask them to compare and contrast the texts. Each child could be asked to think about one or more of the following issues:
- reading 'between the lines';
- the kind of emotive language used;
- the tone of the piece;
- whether the layout affects the writing;
- how the audience/reader is addressed;
- the viewpoint from which the piece is written;
- what the journalist is trying to get across;
- bias.

Give the children plenty of time for reading and discussion. They will soon see how the viewpoint of the journalist and the expected audience changes the way in which the text is written.

Follow-up
Make up an event or situation and get the children to write their own reports of it in different newspaper styles.

Reproducible material

Word bracelets, see page 8

Reading box, see page 21

Class _____

Reading Box Specials

Next week we are going to be focusing on

_____

_____

We will need

_____

_____

Can you help?

If you are sending books or other material that should be returned to you please fill in the bottom of this sheet.

Child's name: _____

Title(s) of book(s) _____ _____ _____

Read-a-day calendar, see page 23

Sunday	Monday	Tuesday	Wednesday	Thursday	Friday	Saturday
1 Make a bookmark	**2** Share a story	**3** Read a chapter of a new book	**4** Listen to someone read	**5** Read a newspaper story	**6** Read a comic	**7** Read a graph
8 Read six advertisements	**9** Read a map	**10** Read a joke to someone	**11** Read a cereal packet	**12** Read a food tin	**13** Read a recipe	**14** Read a game instruction
15 Read some street signs	**16** Read a dictionary	**17** Read a thesaurus	**18** Read some of the telephone directory	**19** Read the instructions for a computer program	**20** Read the TV programme list	**21** Read a holiday brochure
22 Read a science book	**23** Read a poem	**24** Read a video box	**25** Read a letter	**26** Read to a friend	**27** Read the weather forecast	**28** Read some shop window signs
29 Read a magazine	**30** Read an atlas	**31** Read a menu				

Paired reading, see page 52

Use this page to help your friend with his or her reading. As you fill in the blanks, think about the kind of advice that you would like to get to help you do a better job.

1. Name of the listener: _____

2. Name of the reader: _____

3. Date: _____

4. Title of reading: _____

5. Kind of reading (tick one box):

   ☐ poem ☐ report ☐ story ☐ other (tell what kind)

6. Describe what you liked best about the reading. (If you need more space, write on the back.)

   _____

   _____

7. Speed (tick one box). The reader spoke:

   ☐ too quickly ☐ too slowly ☐ just right

8. Volume (tick one box). The reader spoke:

   ☐ too loudly ☐ too softly ☐ just right

9. Clarity (tick one box). The reader's words were:

   ☐ very clear ☐ clear ☐ not clear enough

10. What other helpful advice do you have for the reader? _____

   _____

Reading diaries, see page 75

Book or story title _____

Author _____

Publisher _____

I began reading this book on _____

It took me _____

This is what I liked about the book: _____

I would award _____

for merit out of _____

This picture shows _____

This page may be copied for use in the classroom and should not be declared in any return in respect of any photocopying licence.

Write a picture strip, see page 76

Read-a-thon, see page 79

READ-A-THON SPONSOR SHEET

Name _____

Class _____

School _____

Minimum number of pages to read _____

Sponsor	Address	Amount per page	Number of pages read

Read-a-thon, see page 79

READ-A-THON RECOMMENDATION SHEET

Name _____

Class _____

School _____

Title of book _____

Author _____

Number of pages _____

This book is rated:

☐ Not to be missed! ☐ Enjoyable ☐ OK ☐ Boring

Recommendation: Should this book be bought for the school library?

Why or why not? _____

_____

_____

_____

Discussion club, see page 83

DISCUSSION CLUB REPORT

Date: _____

Your name: _____

The others in your group: _____

Title of the book you discussed: _____

Did anyone read aloud from the book?

☐ Yes   ☐ No

What things did people say about the book? _____

How many people liked the book? _____

How many didn't? _____

Did your group listen to each other

☐ all the time?   ☐ some of the time?   ☐ not at all?

Give your ideas for making the next Discussion Club meeting better: _____

Script-wise, see page 86

NARRATIVE TEXT

The visit to Bordesley Abbey

Cheers went up as the school coach arrived at the site of the old abbey. Class 6 were on their summer trip. They'd been sitting on the coach for hours – well, that was what it seemed like – and they couldn't wait to jump off and stretch their legs.

All except Daniel and Sophie, sitting at the back. The pair of them were bored stiff. An archaeological dig was not their idea of fun!

'Moles,' Mr Branson, their class teacher, droned on. 'Moles dig up the earth and bring all sorts of stuff to the surface....'

But his words were lost to Daniel and Sophie, lagging behind as the others all climbed the stile into the meadow with great excitement.

'Boring,' said Daniel. 'Boring. Boring. Boring.'

PLAYSCRIPT

Scene: The class of children are leaving the coach at the entrance to the abbey where they've arrived on their summer day trip. Daniel, 11, and Sophie, 11, get left behind as the rest of the children file behind their teacher across the field.

Daniel: I s'pose it's a nice day really – pity it's so boring. Look! From this edge of a field you can see the museum where the dig is. In a kind of dip in the meadows.

Sophie: Oh – it's lovely! Look at all the sheep – Daniel look at all the sheep...

Daniel: Sheep!

Sophie: ...and caravans! What are the caravans for? Holidays?

Daniel: Don't be daft! People doing the dig, I suppose. They've got to sleep somewhere, haven't they?

Sophie: I thought they just came and did a bit of digging and went...

Daniel: Nah – they're all students, come and dig in their holidays. And they don't dig. Not real digging! They uncover it slowly, with brushes, paint brushes and things, little tiny bits at a time...

Sophie: Oh, right. Carefully. So they don't disturb anything.

Daniel: S'right. Come on, let's catch the others up.

Sophie: What's this?

Daniel: A stile – come on there's another one across the field... and the others are all down by the river now...

(The children climb across a stile, jump off, and begin to cross the field.)

Sophie: Mr Branson was right about the moles – there must be loads of them. Look! Molehills everywhere...

Character questionnaire, see page 92

Book title: _____

Author: _____

My chosen character is: _____

Character traits	Evidence

Plot chart, see page 99

Book title: _____ **Author:** _____	
Somebody **S**	
Wanted **W**	
But **B**	
So **S**	

Report-a-story, see page 100

Title: _____

Author: _____

What type of book is it?

☐ adventure   ☐ animal   ☐ mystery   ☐ science fiction

☐ other

Describe the plot. What problem or event starts the story? Explain what happens at the end. List a few important or exciting events.

Describe the hero, the villain and other main characters. Say something important about each character's appearance and behaviour.

Describe the setting of the story.

Compare the book with another by the same author. Which one do you think is better? Why?

Rate the book from 0 (terrible) to 10 (terrific) by circling a number.

0   1   2   3   4   5   6   7   8   9   10

Name: _____   Date: _____

Story triangle, see page 101

Book title: ______________________________

Author: ______________________________

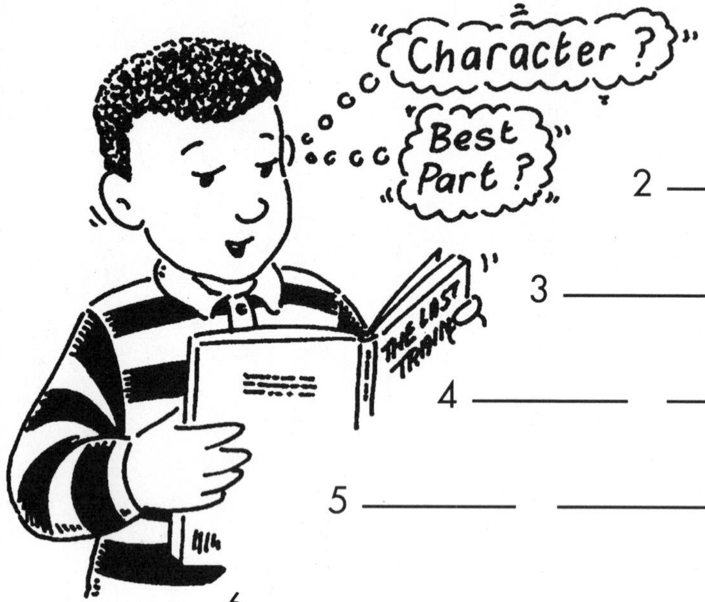

Character ?
Best Part ?
THE LAST TRAIN

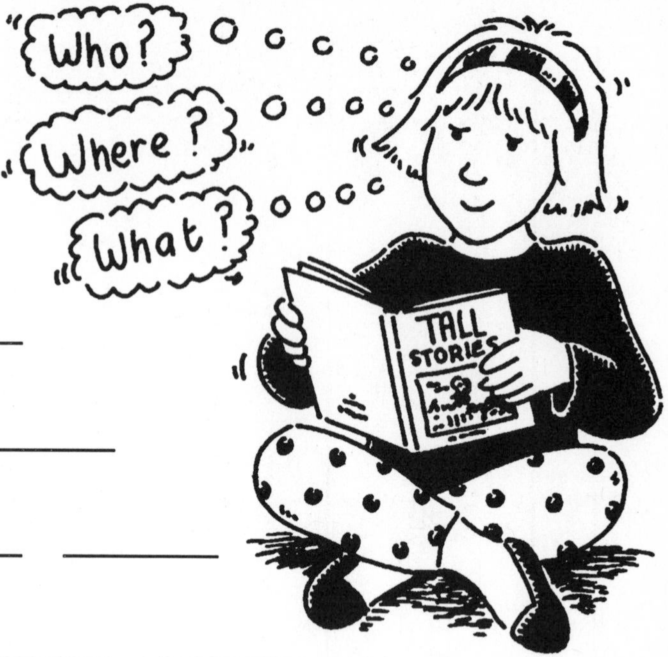

Who?
Where ?
What ?
TALL STORIES

1 ______

2 ______ ______

3 ______ ______ ______

4 ______ ______ ______ ______

5 ______ ______ ______ ______ ______

6 ______ ______ ______ ______ ______ ______

7 ______ ______ ______ ______ ______ ______ ______

8 ______ ______ ______ ______ ______ ______ ______ ______

My name is: ______________________________

I read this story on: ______________________________

One word to describe it: ______________________________

The great book prize, see page 110

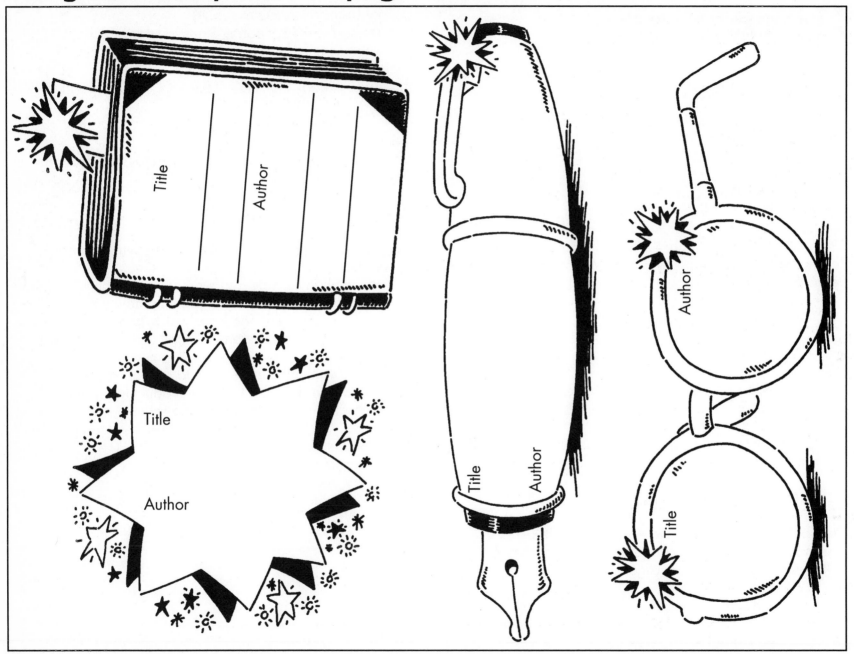

Title
Author

Title
Author

Title
Author

Title

Author

Resources

Word pattern books

Ahlberg, Allan & Janet *Each Peach Pear Plum* (Viking Kestrel)
Burningham, John *Would You Rather...?* (Fontana Picture Lions)
Campbell, Rod *Dear Zoo* (Picture Puffin)
Campbell, Rod *It's Mine* (Picture Piper)
Hutchins, Pat *Goodnight, Owl!* (Bodley Head)
Ormerod, Jan *Come Back, Kittens* (Walker Books)
Rosen, Michael & Oxenbury, Helen *We're Going On A Bear Hunt* (Walker Books)

Wordless books

Carle, Eric *Do You Want To Be My Friend?* (Hamish Hamilton)
Dupasquier, Philippe *I Can't Sleep* (Walker Books)
Ormerod, Jan *Sunshine* (Viking)
Robinson, Colin *Sunrise* (Blackie)
Tafuri, Nancy *Have You Seen My Duckling?* (Picture Puffin)
Wildsmith, Brian *The Apple Bird* (O.U.P)

Useful addresses

The United Kingdom Reading Association (UKRA)
Enquiries c/o Edge Hill College of Higher Education, St. Helens Road, Ormskirk, Lancs.

International Reading Association (IRA)
Enquiries to IRA Headquarters, 800 Barksdale Road, Newark, Delaware 19711, USA

School Library Association (SLA)
Enquiries to 29–31 George Street, Oxford OX1 2AY

National Book League (NBL)
Enquiries to Book House, 45 East Hill, Wandsworth, SW18 2HZ

Centre for the Teaching of Reading
University of Reading School of Education, 29 Eastern Avenue, Reading RG1 5RU

Poets in school

This scheme is run by the Poetry Society with sponsorship by W.H. Smith.

If you would like a poet to work with your children, write a letter to the Poetry Society explaining how you think the visits will benefit them. The letter needs to be sent at the beginning of the term before the term in which you want the poet's visit.

The poet will make three visits to school and, in addition, you will receive £50.00 towards producing an anthology of the children's resulting work. The scheme works on a 'first come, first served' basis, so prepare your letter early!

For full details of this scheme, contact:
The Education Officer
The Poetry Society
22 Betterton Street
London WC2H 9BU